CONSERVATIVE
VICTORY

ALSO BY SEAN HANNITY

Deliver Us from Evil

Let Freedom Ring

CONSERVATIVE VICTORY

Defeating Obama's Radical Agenda

SEAN HANNITY

HARPER

NEW YORK • LONDON • TORONTO • SYDNEY

HARPER

HarperCollins books may be purchased for educational, business, or sales promotional use. For information, please write: Special Markets Department, HarperCollins Publishers, 10 East 53rd Street, New York, NY 10022.

Designed by Jaime Putorti

Library of Congress Cataloging-in-Publication Data is available upon request.

ISBN 978-0-06-200305-8
ISBN 978-0-06-201000-1 (signed edition)

10 11 12 13 14 DIX/RRD 10 9 8 7 6 5 4 3 2 1

Once more:
To my wife, Jill, the love of my life;
And to the greatest gift God ever gave me—
Our two children, Patrick and Merri Kelly

And also for our brave troops,
who put themselves in harm's way
to defend our freedoms,
and for their families

CONTENTS

INTRODUCTION

As harsh as Democrats and the liberal grass roots were in their eight straight years of attacks on George W. Bush and his administration, they had one thing right: There is a great philosophical divide that splits this nation in half—a divide born of diametrically opposite worldviews, which are engaged in an ongoing power struggle over the direction of this nation. This struggle is as old as the United States, but it has grown more intense with each passing decade.

One man who understood this divide, and what it meant for our country, was Ronald Reagan. In a celebrated speech to the Conservative Political Action Conference (CPAC) in 1974, Ronald Reagan described the ideological rift he perceived in America. He warned his listeners of the efforts one side was making to denigrate the nation, its venerated institutions, and the very concept of free-market capitalism, and called attention to that side's goal—to expand government control as a cure for everything that ailed the United States. Though the Vietnam War was nearing its end, Reagan recognized that the stirrings of protest over that conflict had spread far deeper into the culture of the left—and particularly into the universities that were preparing our children for adulthood:

> The widespread disaffection with things military is only a part of the philosophical division in our land today. I must say to you who have recently, or presently are still receiving an education, I am awed by your powers of resistance. I have some knowledge of the attempts that have been made in many classrooms and lecture halls to persuade you that there is little to admire in America. For the second time in this century, capitalism and free enterprise are under assault. Privately owned business is blamed for spoiling the environment, exploiting the worker and seducing, if not outright raping, the customer. Those who make the charge have the solution, of course—government regulation and control.[1]

History repeats itself. That passage could have been lifted from any mainstream conservative publication today. Decades after Reagan's speech, the American left remains deeply suspicious of our military—from Senator John Kerry (D-Mass) accusing our soldiers of terrorizing Iraqi women and children in their homes;[2] to Senator Dick Durbin (D-Ill.) likening our treatment of enemy combatant prisoners at Guantanamo Bay prison to "Nazis, Soviets in their gulags or some other mad regime—Pol Pot or others—that had no concern for human beings";[3] to Congressman John Murtha (D-PA) starting a witch hunt against certain marines after an incident in the Iraqi city of Haditha, in which a number of Iraqi citizens were killed; to Moveon.org demonizing General David Petraeus in a full-page *New York Times* ad as "General Betray Us."[4]

America's leftists have consistently betrayed their disdain for the military, for American exceptionalism, for capitalism and capitalists. But today they've taken their assaults to a new level. It's no exaggeration to say that our future as a nation of liberty and prosperity, and as the world's sole superpower, has never been in greater jeopardy. We are in a war for our national survival. We are in desperate need for a new vision, and an effective strategy, to defeat Barack Obama and the American left before they rob from us everything our ancestors sacrificed to bequeath us, and all that our military has fought, bled, and died to preserve.

In the past, Democrats often managed to downplay the extent of their radicalism, pretending—at least when it suited their political purposes—to be a party of moderates. Thus, while they staunchly opposed the war in Iraq, they insisted that they supported the "good war" in Afghanistan, and in any event, that they always supported our troops. They professed to be on board in the war on terror, even as they sabotaged our intelligence efforts; they pretended to be deficit hawks, even as their policy agenda invariably called for higher deficits than George W. Bush in his worst fiscal year; and they told us they wanted to make abortions "safe, legal and rare," even as they vigorously promoted the culture of death, including that of the unborn.

But in January 2009, when Democrats took firm control of the federal executive and legislative branches, the left had the confidence (and arrogance) to undertake, aggressively and unapologetically, the most ambitious socialistic agenda in this nation's history, including FDR's New Deal. The new president, Barack Obama, still paid lip service to the importance of capitalism. But even as he did so, he unleashed a wide-ranging series of policies that aggregated enormous power to the federal government. Before long, the only ones who believed him anymore were the hopelessly brainwashed yellow-dog Democrats.

The truth is, we are a center-right nation. We treasure our freedoms, our capitalist system, and the way of life that our military sacrifices every day to protect. So it's too bad that more of us didn't take Obama at his word when he promised "fundamental change" for this country—or when he told Joe the Plumber that he wanted to "spread the wealth around a little." For wealth redistribution was precisely the kind of fundamental change he had in mind: a complete restructuring of the American economy, with a dramatic increase in federal control at the expense of the free market and private sector.

Equally alarming, Obama launched his own personal mission to reverse this nation's foreign policy, to make amends for what he misperceived as America's "imperialism," "unilateralism," "arrogance," and "dismissiveness" toward other nations. Under his reign, he decided, tyrants and statesmen alike should realize that we had repented and atoned for pushing our weight around in defiance of world opinion. America would become loved and respected again in the international community.

But Obama's delusions of omnipotence didn't last long. Only months into his presidency, he had so infuriated average Americans that a series of Tea Party protests emerged across the nation, attended by everyday people who were outraged and horrified by Obama's every decision: his reckless federal spending, his seizure of control of private industry, his cap-and-trade legislation, and his obsessive quest to nationalize one-sixth of the American economy through socialized health care.

It was gratifying to watch as grassroots Americans awakened from their apathy and slumber to confront a president who was betraying their way of life. But it's less comforting to realize that Obama and his leftist congressional stablemates have not yet been deterred by the popular backlash against their radical agenda. If anything, they've been emboldened to press harder to impose upon this nation their vision for America—a vision that couldn't be more inconsistent with that of this country's founding fathers or the constitution they crafted.

Instead of listening to the voice of the people, the administration labeled the protestors as "domestic terrorists." Instead of reconsidering his prohibitively expensive cap-and-trade laws, Obama defiantly attended a summit in Copenhagen to work on an international framework to cede our sovereignty to international bodies and transfer wealth to poorer nations in order to right our alleged environmental wrongs. Even in the face of the environmental movements' disgrace over the intercepted email revelations known as Climategate, Obama's EPA unilaterally put forth new regulations that declared even the air we exhale to be a dangerous, toxic substance.

To be sure, Obama maintained the ruse that he was open to alternative solutions. When unemployment rose above 10 percent in December 2009, he opportunistically convened a "jobs summit" at the White House to "hear" ideas about jump-starting job creation—apparently hoping we'd forget his promise that the stimulus package would keep unemployment under 8 percent. But the people who attended his summit weren't the everyday American businesspeople who drive this country: The invitees were mostly ivory-tower intellectuals from academia and government, union leaders in the tank for Obama, and a carefully selected group of business leaders who were already on board to reinforce the agenda he had preordained: a continuation of his failed Keynesian economic mythology. Notably absent were Obama's domestic critics: representatives of the U.S. Chamber of Commerce, the National Federation of Independent Business, or members of any conservative think tanks.[5]

If there were any doubt that Obama intended to stay the course with his profligate spending practices, he put it to rest when he proposed to intercept a large portion of the banks' TARP repayment funds for other purposes. Instead of reducing the indebtedness created by TARP, he wanted to use those funds for a second stimulus package.[6] Rather than learning from his failed policies, he set out to expand them. Rather than responding to the real fear that his debt explosion struck in the heart of most Americans, he brazenly turned a deaf ear and pressed forward with his hugely unpopular[7] quest to nationalize our health care, proving he was anything but a president of the people. Obama's rhetorical overtures to democracy, it turned out, were just a decoy to conceal his unwavering determination to govern from the far left.

Obama's failure to pass his vaunted environmental legislation or his initial attempts at socialized medicine—despite his supermajorities in Congress—did nothing to shake his resolve. Nor did the plummeting of his approval ratings to a point lower than any modern president at that point in his term.[8] He was determined to advance his agenda by any means necessary, including bribing individual congressmen with federal monies directed exclusively to their states. He seemed desperate to implement as much of his agenda as possible before the 2010 and 2012 elections, hoping his changes would be too entrenched to be reversed even with a complete shift in party control.

He also used gimmicks to facilitate passage of his agenda. One of his tactics was to have his legislation passed into law today, but arrange for only parts of it to be effective immediately, with other parts—the hard parts—kicking in after his reelection was secure. We saw just that with his health-care proposals, whose profligate spending requirements wouldn't kick in for some five years, and the cap-and-trade measure, which imposed initially modest, but ever-escalating and burdensome, environmental regulations. Even many of the programs created under his stimulus bill are expected to last long beyond their advertised duration, further expanding government in perpetuity.

Though Obama—helped along by his liberal media—has craftily concealed some of the inevitable pain his legislation will bring, the American people have started catching on, in numbers far larger than even the impressive Tea Party protests would indicate. And they've begun actively opposing his agenda.

But opposition alone—without direction and without organization—could end up playing into Obama's hands. If we're not careful, our grassroots energy could be channeled in ways that could ultimately benefit Obama's cause.

Take, for example, the talk of starting a third party.

It's an understandable impulse: Conservative Americans have been frustrated for years by the Republican establishment's inability to get the country—and Washington—moving in the right direction.

But if all this anger should result in the formation of a third party, the conservative vote could splinter so badly that the White House ends up being delivered back to Obama, however unpopular he has become and however clearly his policies have failed. Yes, the leadership of the Republican Party has often been disappointing—spending too much when in power, and failing to oppose Democrats effectively when out of power. But we all agree that any Republican leadership is vastly superior to the disastrous Democratic policies we've seen in just this first year of Obama's presidency. The differences between the parties are differences in kind, not just degree. And, while the GOP needs to improve its performance, we cannot lose sight of our first priority—to direct the party back to its conservative roots.

We cannot allow the perfect to be the enemy of the good.

This is not to say we'll compromise our principles. We are conservatives; we know what we stand for; and we all realize that the fate of our nation hangs in the balance. But it *is* to say that our best chance to implement policies that are consistent with our principles is to revitalize the Republican Party. To break off into a third party would fracture the conservative movement, leading to years of infighting about policy. It would force millions of Americans to decide whether to stay with the party that historically shared their principles, or abandon it for an organization whose future would be uncertain at best. And it would guarantee Obama's reelection.

Here again, the example of Ronald Reagan shows us the proper path for disgruntled conservatives—conservatives who have become disgusted with the lukewarm, Democrat-lite, Republican-in-name-only (RINO) approach of the GOP leadership. In another speech to the CPAC, on February 6, 1977, Reagan addressed the same dilemma on the heels of his unsuccessful effort to capture the Republican presidential nomination from the GOP establishment candidate, President Gerald Ford. Despite calls from conservatives for him to break with the party, Reagan's message was clear:

> What will be the political vehicle by which the majority can assert its rights? I have to say I cannot agree with some of my friends—perhaps including some of you here tonight— who have answered that question by saying this nation needs a new political party. I respect that view and I know that those

who have reached it have done so after long hours of study. But I believe that political success of the principles we believe in can best be achieved in the Republican Party. I believe the Republican Party can hold and should provide the political mechanism through which the goals of the majority of Americans can be achieved. For one thing, the biggest single grouping of conservatives is to be found in that party. It makes more sense to build on that grouping than to break it up and start over.

Rather than a third party, we can have a new first party made up of people who share our principles. I have said before that if a formal change in name proves desirable, then so be it. But tonight, for purpose of discussion, I'm going to refer to it simply as the New Republican Party. And let me say so there can be no mistakes as to what I mean: The New Republican Party I envision will not be, and cannot be limited to the country club–big business image that, for reasons both fair and unfair, it is burdened with today.

The New Republican Party I am speaking about is going to have room for the man and the woman in the factories, for the farmer, for the cop on the beat and the millions of Americans who may never have thought of joining our party before, but whose interests coincide with those represented by principled Republicanism. If we are to attract more working men and women of this country, we will do so not by simply "making room" for them, but by making certain they have a say in what goes on in the party. The Democratic Party turned its back on the majority of social conservatives during the 1960s. The New Republican Party of the late '70s and '80s must welcome them, seek them out, enlist them, not only as rank-and-file members but as leaders and as candidates.

What was true in 1977 remains true today. Now, as then, the Republican Party is still home to the American conservative movement. Though the party has sometimes lost its way, its platform and body of principles remain strong—strong enough to survive even when its leaders momentarily lose sight of those principles.

The conservative movement has some counterfeit well-wishers in the liberal media, and others who are, in truth, liberal-lite conservatives. They contend that the only way for the Republican Party to regain its electoral majority is to move toward the center. It must moderate its positions, lest it lose forever its appeal to independent voters.

But the highway to the kind of big-tent Republicanism that Ronald Reagan espoused does not lead through the land of Democrat-lite. If we allow the left to set the agenda—if we agree to compete with them on their terms—the outcome will always be the same: Democratic victories and the advancement of the liberal agenda. We can establish new entitlement programs, we can raise taxes, we can boast of our enlightened multiculturalism, but no matter how far we go in that direction—God forbid!—it will never be enough.

No, the way to extend the Republican tent to every American is to return to first principles—to America's founding principles. It is to articulate these ideas unapologetically, and in a matter that conveys their natural appeal to mainstream Americans, just as Ronald Reagan did.

If we should succumb to the temptation to form a third party, we would be handing Barack Obama the greatest gift he could ever imagine. And, at the risk of sounding dramatic, we could be furnishing the final nail in the coffin of this republic.

Instead we need to reconnect with what conservatism means.

We need to demonstrate that conservative values are inherently more compassionate than liberal thinking. And we need to remind ourselves that, as history shows, conservative leadership is the best path to economic prosperity and national security.

We can learn from another historical parallel from the late 1970s—the Carter years. During Jimmy Carter's presidency, liberalism was in the driver's seat, and it wreaked havoc on every policy highway. Those years are infamous for their air of malaise, for the so-called "misery index" that measured the failure of Carter's domestic policies (out-of-control inflation, interest rates, and unemployment), and for the perception that the nation had gone soft, weak—a demilitarized America in retreat on foreign policy.

Jimmy Carter's four years in office were one long rude awakening. And, after his stunning victory and near-deification in the 2008 election, Barack Obama must have felt much the same way in the past year, as reality set in and he discovered that most Americans didn't share his jaundiced view of pre-Obama America, or his disdain for free enterprise, American exceptionalism, and rugged individualism.

Since he took office, Obama's unabashed liberalism has been on display for all to see—and it's not pretty. It's grounded in a set of false assumptions about the human condition as well as about America's founding principles. Just as they did during the Carter years, Americans are beginning to see how dangerously liberal today's Democratic Party truly is. They are eager to consolidate around a revitalized Republican Party—a party characterized by policies of bold colors, not pale pastels.

In the first year of the Obama administration, congressional Republicans have been forced to serve as the Party of No: With the hyperpartisan, ultramilitant Democratic supermajorities in

Congress, it would be pure fantasy to imagine that any of the GOP's positive ideas could make it past the congressional starting blocks. But soon the party will have to present an aggressive, alternative agenda, grounded in conservative principles and centered on individual liberty—a concept that has been totally forgotten by the Beltway power elite. If we don't soon break this suicidal cycle of cradle-to-grave security, we may pass the tipping point and find that our individual liberties are irretrievably lost.

Later in this book, I'll have more to say about why a revitalized Republican Party is the only realistic vehicle to stop the Obama train wreck, about the principles around which our new party must organize, and about the strategy to convert this new party into a sustained, winning majority.

But the first step we must take, as we organize and rally our "troops," is to review what is at stake. In Part One, we'll explore why the triumph of our ideas, over those of the Obama leftists, is of paramount importance. We'll examine Obama's political roots and his leftist mentorship and associations—not to condemn him unfairly, but to illustrate that his policies are an outgrowth of the radicalism that is deeply ingrained in his political being. This background will help us recognize any false overtures toward compromise he may extend, and help us resist being lulled into relaxing our guard.

We'll explore Obama's training in the street-agitation tactics of Saul Alinsky—conducted in the guise of "community organizing"—and how he uses these techniques today to implement the kind of "fundamental change" he wants to see in our national fabric, all from his perch of power in the Oval Office. We'll dig deeper into his agenda, both its domestic and foreign policy components, and see that it cannot reasonably be confused for anything other than hardcore leftist ideology. And before long it will be clear how all the pieces fit together: that a thread of leftist extremism runs through Barack Obama's entire life, from his mysterious distant past, to his days as a community organizer, to his state senate days in Illinois, to the United States Senate, and to his dangerous presidency.

PART I

Why Victory Is So Important

ONE

OBAMA'S HISTORY OF RADICALISM

When it comes to Barack Obama's now well-known history of associating with far-left radicals, I can modestly say I was way ahead of the curve. During the 2008 presidential campaign, I took some criticism for probing the past of this little-known candidate. But I trust that now most can see the relevance of the associations he has made throughout his life, and how they've shaped the policies he pursues today. The connection is undeniable.

On February 28, 2007, I pointed out a discrepancy that troubled me. The media had been making great hay over Mitt Romney's affiliation with the Mormon Church. But little interest had been shown in candidate Barack Obama's membership in a different religious organization: the Trinity Unity Church in Chicago. At a time when we knew little about Obama's past—other than what he'd revealed in his own writings—it struck me that this chapter in Obama's past deserved deeper scrutiny.

That night I interviewed columnist Erik Rush, who had written a piece on Obama and his church.

In his piece, Rush pointed out that the biography appearing

on Obama's official U.S. Senate website disclosed that he and his family "live on Chicago's South Side where they attend Trinity United Church of Christ." When Rush checked into that church, however, he discovered that this was no conventional American religious gathering. Trinity, he wrote, was "not simply afrocentric, it's African-centric. In fact, one could argue this organization worships things African to a far greater degree than they do Christ, and gives the impression of being a separatist 'church' in the same vein as do certain supremacist 'white brethren' churches—or even Louis Farrakhan's Nation of Islam."[9]

Rush cited the church's mission statement, which was displayed on its website (www.tucc.org):

> We are a congregation which is Unashamedly Black and Unapologetically Christian. . . . Our roots in the Black religious experience and tradition are deep, lasting and permanent. We are an African people, and remain "true to our native land," the mother continent, the cradle of civilization. God has superintended our pilgrimage through the days of slavery, the days of segregation, and the long night of racism. It is God who gives us the strength and courage to continuously address injustice as a people, and as a congregation. We constantly affirm our trust in God through cultural expression of a Black worship service and ministries which address the Black Community.
>
> Trinity United Church of Christ adopted the Black Value System written by the Manford Byrd Recognition Committee chaired by Vallmer Jordan in 1981. We believe in the following 12 precepts and covenantal statements. These Black Ethics must be taught and exemplified in homes, churches, nurseries and schools, wherever Blacks are gathered. They must reflect the following concepts:

1. Commitment to God
2. Commitment to the Black Community
3. Commitment to the Black Family
4. Dedication to the Pursuit of Education
5. Dedication to the Pursuit of Excellence
6. Adherence to the Black Work Ethic
7. Commitment to Self-Discipline and Self-Respect
8. Disavowal of the Pursuit of "Middleclassness"
9. Pledge to make the fruits of all developing and acquired skills available to the Black Community
10. Pledge to Allocate Regularly, a Portion of Personal Resources for Strengthening and Supporting Black Institutions
11. Pledge allegiance to all Black leadership who espouse and embrace the Black Value System
12. Personal commitment to embracement of the "Black Value System."

Rush added that the church's vision "more resembles a cult than a church. Only this one has as one of its most prominent members a serious contender for the White House."

These weren't my personal assessments, keep in mind: They were Rush's reporting, based on the characterizations of church insiders themselves. The *Chicago Tribune* reported that "Vallmer Jordan, a church member who helped draft the [church's] precepts, said they were designed to empower the black community and counter a value system imposed by whites." [10]

During my interview with Erik Rush, I said to him, "You know, if there were a presidential candidate, and they were part of [this] church—and, as you point out in your column, you substitute[d] the word 'black' for the word 'white'—there would be an outrage in this country. There would be cries of racism in this country." [11] And I meant it. It was troubling to find that a serious presidential candidate had long attended a church that seemed so racially oriented.

The following night, I interviewed the pastor of the church, Dr. Jeremiah Wright. I wanted to get to the bottom of this issue and find out if the church was as race-centered as its precepts made it sound—and, if so, why Barack Obama would attend such a church.

I opened the interview with direct questions, citing the church's tenets and asking Reverend Wright whether he believed that, if another church had adopted those tenets but had substituted "white" for "black," we would call that church racist.

Without skipping a beat, and certainly without apology, Wright responded: "No, we would call it Christianity. We've been saying that since there was a white Christianity; we've been saying that ever since Christians took part in the slave trade; we've been saying that ever since they had churches in slave castles. We don't have to say the word 'white.' We just have to live in white America, the United States of white America. That's not the issue; you're missing the issue."

As I tried to pursue my line of questioning, Reverend Wright cut me off, telling me that Erik Rush "doesn't know anything more about theology than I know about brain surgery. . . . If you're not going to talk about theology in context, if you're not going to talk about liberation theology that came out of the 1960s . . . black liberation theology, that started with Jim Cone in 1968, and the writings of Cone, and the writings of Dwight Hopkins, and the writings of womanist theologians, and Asian theologians, and Hispanic theologians . . . [Once you've done that,] then you can talk about the black value system."

As we continued, Reverend Wright seemed to grow increasingly combative. He kept bringing up the writings of Cone and Hopkins, suggesting, in effect, that unless I was familiar with their theological writings I couldn't understand, much less intelligently discuss, the church's theology. "Let me suggest that you do some reading before you come and talk to me about my field," he scolded.

When my cohost, Alan Colmes, picked up the conversation, Wright basically admitted that his church was African-centered. But he denied that that carried any suggestion of superiority or separatism. "It assumes Africans speaking for themselves as subjects in history, not objects in history."

"MARXISM DRESSED UP AS CHRISTIANITY"

In the course of our exchange, Reverend Wright had advised me to read up on several things—Black Liberation Theology, and the writings of James Cone and Dwight Murphy—and I took him up on his advice.

As the *New York Times* reported in a piece on Obama and Wright, Black Liberation Theology, as its name suggests, is a race-centered theology—one that "interprets the Bible as the story of the struggles of black people, who by virtue of their oppression, are better able to understand Scripture than those who have suffered less." [12]

In the *Concise Dictionary of Christian Theology*, we learn that Black Liberation Theology is one of the several liberation theologies that put "more emphasis on deliverance of human beings from various types of temporal bondage—economic, political, and social—than on personal redemption from sin. It tends to draw upon social sciences rather than biblical and theological bases." Also known simply as "black theology," it "regards God's concern for the salvation of humans as not being exclusively spiritually oriented, but as also pertaining to political, economic, and social deliverance. James Cone is the major theologian of the movement." The *Moody Handbook of Theology* illuminates that idea further: "According to Cone, Jesus did not come to bring spiritual liberation but to liberate the oppressed."

The more I read about this theology, the more it became clear how politically, socially, and economically driven—rather than spiritually driven—it is. The *Moody Handbook of Theology* describes the broader category of "liberation theology," of which Black Liberation Theology is a type: It does not "approach the concepts of God, Christ, man, sin, and salvation from an orthodox, biblical perspective, but reinterprets them in a political context." [13]

Many argue that adherents of this theology tend toward a Marxist worldview and harbor a disdain for capitalism and capitalist systems. Writing in the *National Review,* Stanley Kurtz has pointed out that "a scarcely concealed, Marxist-inspired indictment of American capitalism pervades contemporary 'black-liberation theology' "—a point Erik Rush also made in his piece on Obama. And Reverend Wright, it turned out, had quite a number of troubling associations with other radical figures: He had publicly hailed Reverend Louis Farrakhan, and in 1984 even traveled to Libya with Farrakhan to visit Colonel Muammar Qaddafi.

One writer who was concerned about Obama's church was Kyle-Anne Shiver, a writer for *American Thinker*. After making her own study of the tenets of Black Liberation Theology—which she likened to "Marxism dressed up to look like Christianity"— she visited Trinity United herself and was more surprised by the church bookstore than by Wright's controversial preaching, which she had already witnessed on video. Having visited some one hundred Christian bookstores before, she said that there was one common denominator among all the books for sale: *Christianity*. That was not the case with the Trinity store. There, instead, she was surprised to find as many Muslim—specifically, Black Muslim—books as Christian ones. Even the books that were Christian-oriented, she said, were more political than religious, such as those by James Cone. The theme that tied those books together, she concluded, was neither Christianity nor any other real religion, but Marxist philosophy.[14]

Even those passingly familiar with Black Liberation Theology would find it difficult to deny that it promotes racial deliverance even above Christ-centeredness. As its godfather, James Cone, wrote in his treatise *Black Theology and Power*:

> As in 1969, I still regard Jesus Christ today as the chief focus of my perspective on God but not to the exclusion of other religious perspectives. God's reality is not bound by one manifestation of the divine in Jesus but can be found wherever people are being empowered to fight for freedom. Life-giving power for the poor and the oppressed is the primary criterion that we must use to judge the adequacy of our theology, not abstract concepts. As Malcolm X put it: "I believe in a religion that believes in freedom. Any time I have to accept a religion that won't let me fight a battle for my people, I say to hell with that religion."

Yes, Cone does begin by saying that Jesus Christ is "the chief focus of [his] perspective on God." As we read on, however, we see that he contends that Christianity is not exclusive—which runs counter to every Christian principle—and that there are other "manifestations of the divine" on par with Jesus, a notion I find difficult to reconcile with mainstream Christianity, whether Catholic or Protestant. Beyond that, Cone seems to demand that the Christian religion conform to his political beliefs and racial aspirations, not the other way around.

Cone also approvingly quotes Malcolm X invoking the well-known vernacular of Karl Marx:

> The point that I would like to impress upon every Afro-American leader is that there is no kind of action in this country ever going to bear fruit unless that action is tied in with the overall international [class] struggle.

And there is further proof that Cone views Christianity through racial and Marxist lenses. Take, for instance, his blasphemous assertion: "What we need is the divine love as expressed in Black Power, which is the power of Black people to destroy their oppressors here and now by any means at their disposal. *Unless God is participating in this holy activity, we must reject his love*" (emphasis added).[15] Furthermore, writes Cone, if Jesus is not seen as being part of the Marxist class struggle, he must be viewed as a "white Jesus," and they must "destroy him."[16]

Cone viewed liberation not as merely *consistent with* the gospel, but *as* the gospel. "There is, then, a desperate need for a black theology . . . whose sole purpose is to apply the freeing power of the gospel to black people under white oppression."[17] The task of black theology, he said, is "to analyze the nature of the gospel of Jesus Christ in the light of oppressed black people so they will see the gospel as inseparable from their humiliated condition, bestowing on them the necessary power to break the chains of oppression." [18]

For Cone, "black power and black religion are inseparable." [19] Black religion was only authentic when coupled with the struggle for black freedom,[20] such that the black theology of Malcolm X is an indispensable corrective for Christianity.[21]

Why is this important? Because James Cone, the man spewing these thoughts, was the primary spiritual mentor of Reverend Jeremiah Wright—who in turn was the primary spiritual mentor of Barack Obama.

Theologian John S. Feinberg describes liberation theology as one of four main forms of postmodern theology.[22] Feinberg notes that liberation theology took root in Latin America but has spread throughout the world in various forms. "In North America, it has expressed itself as black theology." He describes it as more of a practical than intellectual theology. "As opposed to earlier theologies, whose aim was to reflect on the being and attributes of God or to apply reason to natural and special revelation to discern what can be known about God, liberation theology is concerned with critical reflection on praxis (the practical)."

"AMERICA'S CHICKENS ARE COMING HOME TO ROOST"

Over time I began to look deeper into Reverend Wright's particular beliefs, read some of his writings, and watched some of his taped sermons. I soon concluded that he definitely embraced, wholesale, the tenets of his church, including the Black Value System. I discovered that, in his sermon on the Sunday following the 9/11 attacks, he said the attacks were a consequence of American policies. And that was not just a knee-jerk allegation he would come to regret or retract; four years later, he charged that the attacks were retribution for America's racism.[23]

In one church-affiliated magazine, Wright wrote, "In the 21st century, white America got a wake-up call after 9/11/01. White America and the western world came to realize that people of color had not gone away, faded into the woodwork or just 'disappeared' as the Great White West kept on its merry way of ignoring black concerns." In one sermon, his message was even more pointed: "Racism is how this country was founded and how this country is still run! . . . We are deeply involved in the importing of drugs, the exporting of guns and the training of professional killers. . . . We believe in white supremacy and black inferiority and believe it more than we believe in God. . . . We conducted radiation experiments on our own people. . . . We care nothing about human life if the ends justify the means! . . . And. And! *And!* God! Has got! To be sick! Of this sh*t!"[24]

The most disturbing of Wright's known diatribes are the sermons in which he cursed America and our heritage. During the campaign, I played clips from these sermons repeatedly, hoping the American electorate would wake up to the mind-set they represented—a mind-set with which Obama had publicly affiliated himself. Even ABC News, in its "review of dozens of Rev. Wright's sermons, offered for sale by the church, found repeated denunciations of the U.S. based on what Wright described as his reading of the Gospels and the treatment of black Americans."[25]

In one well-publicized sermon in 2003, Wright shouted, "The government gives them the drugs, builds bigger prisons, passes a three-strike law and then wants us to sing 'God Bless America.' No, no, no, God *damn* America, that's in the Bible for killing innocent people. God damn America for treating our citizens as less than human. God damn America for as long as she acts like she is God and she is supreme." In another sermon, Wright repeated his charge that America's policies had brought on Al Qaeda's 9/11 attacks against us. He said, "We have supported state terrorism against the Palestinians and black South Africans, and now we are indignant because the stuff we have done overseas is now brought right back to our own front yards. America's chickens are coming home to roost."[26]

Obama and his handlers quickly struggled to distance Obama from Wright. When confronted with the news of the pastor's vitriolic sermons, Obama said he was outraged and appalled—especially by Wright's claim that criticism of his sermons was an attack on the black church, and that the U.S. government was responsible for the AIDS virus. Obama said, "The person I saw yesterday was not the person that I met twenty years ago."[27]

But other voices challenged Obama's claim that there were two different Jeremiah Wrights. John McCormack, writing on the *Weekly Standard* blog, cited paragraphs from Obama's own book *Dreams from My Father*, in which Obama related a Wright sermon from twenty years before.[28] He quoted Wright as saying, "It is this world, a world where cruise ships throw away more food in a day than most residents of Port-au-Prince see in a year, where white folks' greed runs a world in need, apartheid in one hemisphere, apathy in another hemisphere. . . . That's the world! On which hope sits!"

It's hard to deny that Reverend Wright was every bit as bitter two decades ago as he remains today. In an early presidential campaign profile, the *New York Times* chronicled Obama's search for faith and his spiritual initiation at the foot of Wright's fiery, angry pulpit. As the *Times* reported, Obama "was entranced by Mr. Wright, whose sermons fused analysis of the Bible with outrage at what he saw as the racism of everything from daily life in Chicago to American foreign policy." [29]

Obama was moved by this angry, race-centered pastor, who became not just a spiritual mentor, but also a role model. The *Times* says that "services at Trinity were a weekly master class in how to move an audience. When Mr. Obama arrived at Harvard Law School later that year, where he fortified himself with recordings of Mr. Wright's sermons, he was delivering stirring speeches as a student leader in the classical oratorical style of the black church." [30]

In fact, one could fairly say that Wright—the Wright of twenty years ago—was instrumental in Obama's rise to national power. Obama catapulted himself onto the national scene with his "Audacity of Hope" speech at the Democratic National Convention in 2004—a speech he proudly admits was inspired by one of Reverend Wright's sermons. "I actually stole that line ["The audacity of hope"] from my pastor," he told one audience.

> [Wright's] premise was very simple. His premise was that it's actually easier to be cynical. It's easier to assume that the world as it is, is how it must be. . . . The temptation is to take refuge in cynicism and say, I can't do anything about that. . . . What my pastor continued to say then is what requires boldness, what takes risk, what is audacious is to hope—to believe that despite the hardships . . . that somehow we can use our imaginations and our will to create a world that is a little bit better, a little more fair, a little more just, a little more equal than the one that we inherited. [31]

Indeed, Obama's crusade for universal health care was inspired by this same philosophy and call to action. He has drawn that connection himself: "I love that idea in my own life because it didn't call for you to ignore the problems that we have; in fact it insists that you look at them squarely. It insists that if we are spending more money on health care than any nation on earth, why can't we come together and form a plan that provides all our people decent, basic, affordable health care?"

Though Obama eventually threw Wright overboard—as he has so many other people when it became politically expedient—he can never erase the facts: that he voluntarily attended Wright's church for twenty years; that he chose Wright to marry him and his wife; and that he selected Trinity as the church to spiritually nurture his children.

This much was clear: The blueprint for Obama's socialist agenda—based on a grievance mentality—could be found in the writings of his radical spiritual mentor. The writing was on the wall. I did my best, on radio and television, to call attention to the plain facts before me. But not everyone was willing to believe it—not yet.

OBAMA *PICKED* JEREMIAH WRIGHT

In February 2007, Ben Wallace-Wells published an extensive piece on Barack Obama and Reverend Wright in *Rolling Stone*. As he reported, Obama's relationship with Wright was "as openly radical a background as any significant American political figure has ever emerged from, as much Malcolm X as Martin Luther King Jr. Wright is not an incidental figure in Obama's life, or his politics. The senator 'affirmed' his Christian faith in this church; he uses Wright as a 'sounding board' to 'make sure I'm not losing myself in the hype and hoopla.' " Wallace-Wells quoted Reverend Jim Wallis, "a leader of the religious left," as stating, "If you want to understand where Barack gets his feeling and rhetoric from, just look at Jeremiah Wright." Indeed, wrote Wallace-Wells, "Obama wasn't born into Wright's world. . . . Obama could have picked any church. . . . Obama chose Trinity United. He *picked* Jeremiah Wright. Obama wrote in his autobiography that on the day he chose this church, he felt the spirit of black memory and history moving through Wright."[32]

Wallace-Wells cites Obama's two autobiographies, which reinforce the fact that Obama was not just a casual churchgoer, but in fact one who bought wholeheartedly into Wright's message. "When you read his autobiography, the surprising thing—for such a measured politician—is the depth of radical feeling that seeps through, the amount of Jeremiah Wright that's packed in there," Wallace-Wells wrote.

Interestingly, after reading through Obama's books, listening to his speeches, and watching his behavior, I had independently come to the same conclusion about Obama's attitudes toward race. By this point, Team Obama was working overtime to paint him as a postracial candidate, but is this in fact the case? His own writings reveal some very questionable attitudes.

In *Dreams from My Father*, for instance, Obama writes, "I ceased to advertise my mother's race at the age of twelve or thirteen, when I began to suspect that by doing so I was ingratiating myself to whites."[33]

Obama described his own white grandmother as "a typical white person"—"a woman who once confessed her fear of black men who passed by her on the street, and who on more than one occasion has uttered racial or ethnic stereotypes that made me cringe." So what are we to assume from Obama's perspective—other than that a "typical white person" is a racist who fears black men?

And such assumptions have continued to mark Obama's conduct even during his presidency. One notable case was his spontaneous reaction to an altercation between a Cambridge, Massachusetts, police officer and Henry Louis Gates, Jr., a noted African American professor at Harvard University. The conflict occurred when the police arrested Gates for disorderly conduct as they responded to a call to investigate a suspected burglary at his home. When a reporter asked Obama about the incident at a health-care conference, Obama, without knowing all the facts, denounced the police as having acted "stupidly." He defended Gates, hinting that race may have played a role in the arrest, saying that it's "fair to say . . . any of us would be pretty angry." Though he later tried to downplay his own role in inflaming the story by inviting Gates and the arresting officer to a White House "beer summit," that gesture did nothing to alter his pre-judgment of the event—a statement that spoke volumes about his own racial attitude, and one for which he never apologized.

There is also evidence that Obama shares Wright's disdain for America. Wallace-Wells reports that Obama told him, "I'm somebody who believes in this country and its institutions. But I often think they're broken." While part of Obama believes in America's capacity for outstanding virtue, the reporter wrote, he also "feels very deeply that this country's exercise of its great inherited wealth and power has been grossly unjust." [34]

Can Obama truly believe that our nation's wealth and power have been "inherited," rather than being a product of its founding principles and constitutional system? Without a doubt. As Wallace-Wells warned long before Obama was elected, Obama believes America has abused and misused her wealth and power. This belief explains his obsessive riffs against the United States on foreign soil, his incessant apologies for our past behavior, and his assurances that under his reign, America will do better. His conviction that this nation's institutions are broken explains his quest to fundamentally change America—an America that in fact was not broken, at least not before he came to office.

That Obama was steeped in the twisted worldview of Reverend Wright was painfully obvious to anyone following the political scene, and especially to my viewers and listeners. But the mainstream media, other liberals, and the Democratic Party establishment were determined to discount Obama's identification with Wright's racist and anti-American beliefs. They hastened to point out that Obama had criticized Wright for his "inflammatory rhetoric," and said it wasn't fair to judge Obama by association. They accepted, unquestioningly, Obama's ludicrous claim that he had not been present in Wright's church for any sermon in which he had made such statements or expressed such attitudes.

The truth, as Wallace-Wells wrote, is that—of all the other pastors in the Chicago area—Barack Obama *chose* Reverend Wright to follow. He marveled at his theology, and at the oratorical magic Wright brought to bear in service to causes they both believed in. This wasn't guilt by association: Obama had actively embraced Wright. It was a fair charge, and a real concern.

And Wright was by no means the first, or even the dominant influence, on the molding of Obama's radical mind-set. That process started much earlier, with even closer associations. For Obama, his affiliation with Reverend Jeremiah Wright was just a continuation of this pattern of relationships—one that would serve as an affirmation and validation of his already-shaped worldview. As it happens, the radical influences on Obama's life have been interwoven throughout every year of his life. My purpose in highlighting these radical associations during the campaign, and to delve more deeply into them now, is not to smear him, but to understand him—to demonstrate that Obama has a genuinely radical past, one that serves as an accurate predictor of his presidential policy agenda.

A RED DIAPER BABY

If Obama's socialist ideas seem alien to those of us who were raised on American capitalist values, it may come as no surprise that they have deep roots in his upbringing. Unlike nearly any other American politician, Barack Obama spent his formative years in a land where communism was no abstract principle, but a cause that had recently led to a bloody civil war: Indonesia. The media has devoted little effort to inquiring into the impact these formative years had on his political education. But what we know about his background raises troubling, unresolved questions.

Some have speculated that Obama may have been a "red diaper baby,"[35] the child of communist-leaning parents. Certainly his mother, Stanley Ann Dunham, was an iconoclast and a radical thinker; one classmate called her a "fellow traveler."[36] After divorcing Obama's Kenyan father, his mother, known as Ann, moved with her son to Indonesia, the home of her new husband, Lolo Soetoro. Barack Obama lived in Indonesia from ages six to ten, just after a civil war in which the Communist Party of that nation, known as PKI, was obliterated. During this period—and especially in the city of Jarkarta, where the Soetoros lived—PKI members continued to be slaughtered. At such an impressionable age, young Obama must have been profoundly affected by these events.[37]

In *Dreams from My Father*, Obama himself lets slip that, during their time in Indonesia, his mother raised him to be contemptuous of America and Americans. On page 47, Obama describes himself as "extremely well mannered when compared to other American children. She [his mother] had taught me to disdain the blend of ignorance and arrogance that too often characterized Americans abroad."[38] On the same page, Obama relates his mother's refusal to attend social functions with her husband's fellow American oil company employees because "those are not my people."[39] Is it any wonder that Obama spends most of his time abroad today blasting the United States for being "arrogant" and "dismissive" toward other nations and peoples?

After leaving Indonesia in the early 1970s, Obama spent several years in Hawaii. While he was there, his maternal grandfather, Stanley Armour Dunham, introduced Obama to his early mentor, Frank Marshall Davis, an African American journalist, poet, and radical who was known to the FBI in the 1950s as a member of the Communist Party.[40] Davis became like a father to Obama, even advising him on his career decisions.

With such radical early influences, it's inconceivable that Obama wasn't seriously affected by their ideas. He publicly admits that, on a matter as deep and personal as his own religion, he adopted his family's skepticism. "I was not raised in a particularly religious household. . . . My mother grew up with a healthy skepticism of organized religion herself. As a consequence, so did I."[41] And he admits that he counts his mother as "the dominant figure in my formative years," and that "the values she taught me continue to be my touchstone when it comes to how I go about the world of politics."[42]

Throughout his early years, Obama was surrounded by far leftists—from Indonesia to Hawaii to Harvard to Chicago— all of whom embraced an identical political narrative, which viewed the United States, its capitalistic system, its freedom, and its democracy as suspicious at best, satanic at worst.[43] With that background in mind, it becomes clear that Obama's decision to choose Reverend Wright and his Trinity Church was no accident, but the next step in an ideological journey—a spiritual home with which he could comfortably identify.

"DIG IT. MANSON KILLED THOSE PIGS!"

Obama speaks proudly of his years in Chicago, but this activity is not as innocuous as it sounds. This is the venue where Obama was trained by radicals in the methods of the influential leftist organizer Saul Alinsky, and where he began to put this training into practice, serving as an attorney for the Association of Community Organizations for Reform Now (ACORN)—a left-wing activist group that bills itself as a non-profit, non-partisan social justice organization—and training its workers in "community organizing."[44] Alinsky wrote *Rules for Radicals*, a blueprint for Marxist organizing and agitation, and his ruthless, militant strategies are bearing fruit through Obama and his take-no-prisoners allies, from the White House to ACORN to the Service Employees International Union(SEIU).

Tellingly, Saul Alinsky's son, L. David Alinsky, praised Obama in a letter to the *Boston Globe* for utilizing his father's strategies at the 2008 Democratic National Convention:

> The Democratic National Convention had all the elements of the perfectly organized event, Saul Alinsky style. Barack Obama's training in Chicago by the great community organizers is showing its effectiveness. It is an amazingly powerful format, and the method of my late father always works to

get the message out and get the supporters on board. When executed meticulously and thoughtfully, it is a powerful strategy for initiating change and making it really happen. Obama learned his lesson well. I am proud to see that my father's model for organizing is being applied successfully beyond local community organizing to affect the Democratic campaign in 2008. It is a fine tribute to Saul Alinsky as we approach his 100th birthday.[45]

It was in Chicago that Obama formed his first adult associations with far-left political forces—including the radical Weather Underground principal and unrepentant Pentagon bombing terrorist William Ayers;[46] Ayers's radical cohort (and now wife) Bernadine Dohrn; and the Democratic Socialists of America (DSA).

Obama laughably downplays William Ayers—a close associate with whom he served on the board of the Woods Fund of Chicago and who hosted an event at his home launching Obama's state senate run—as just a guy in the neighborhood, a harmless Chicago college professor. During the campaign, he claimed not even to have been aware of Ayers's radical and terrorist past. As RedState's Erick Erickson has observed, however, Obama would have to have ignored local Chicago media entirely in 1996 not to have caught wind of Ayers's inglorious record. To believe Obama was ignorant of Ayers's notoriety—of which the radical professor himself made no secret—requires an acute suspension of disbelief.

What self-respecting patriot, knowing what Obama must have known about Ayers, would go anywhere near such a man, much less break bread and share common cause with him?

Through most of the 2008 campaign, the mainstream media

shamelessly covered up Obama's relationship with Ayers. According to NewsBusters.org, with one small exception, Ayers received virtually no attention from the three broadcast networks. But others, such as Ethics and Public Policy Center senior fellow Stanley Kurtz, exposed the relationship. After reviewing the relevant documents at the Chicago Annenberg Challenge (CAC), Kurtz concluded in an article for the *Wall Street Journal* that Obama and Ayers "worked as a team to advance the CAC agenda," which "flowed from Mr. Ayers's educational philosophy, which called for infusing students and their parents with a radical political commitment, and which downplayed achievement tests in favor of activism." Ayers was quite open about his political agenda: In an interview at around the time the CAC was founded, Kurtz reports, Ayers described himself openly as "a radical, Leftist, small 'c' communist." [47]

Ayers, as we know, hadn't changed his ways from his radical youth. In a profile published by the *New York Times* on September 11, 2001, the day of the terrorist attacks, Ayers expressed no regret for his past as a member of the violent 1960s extremist group the Weather Underground. "I don't regret setting bombs," he told the *Times.* "I feel we didn't do enough." [48] Around that same time, *Chicago* magazine published its own lengthy profile of Ayers, replete with photos—one of which pictured Ayers defiantly standing on an American flag on the ground in an alley.

And Ayers's soulmate, Bernadine Dohrn, had a past that was at least as disturbing as his own. After the infamous Manson family murders in Beverly Hills, California, in 1969, Dohrn told a gathering of the radical Students for a Democratic Society, "Dig it! Manson killed those pigs, then they ate dinner in the same room with them, then they shoved a fork into a victim's stomach." [49] At one time Dohrn was on the FBI's 10 Most Wanted

List; J. Edgar Hoover called her "the most dangerous woman in America."[50]

Throughout the campaign, I continued to hammer home Obama's close relationship with Ayers and Dohrn, just as I had stressed his association with Reverend Wright. But Democrats, liberals, and the mainstream media were uniformly dismissive, responding to each new revelation with the familiar charge of "guilt by association." In fact, the evidence pointed to something different: guilt by participation. As Stanley Kurtz put it, "As CAC chairman, Mr. Obama was lending moral and financial support to Mr. Ayers and his radical circle. That is a story even if Mr. Ayers had never planted a single bomb 40 years ago."[51]

Nor should we ignore Obama's connection with the Democratic Socialists of America (DSA), a socialist group that endorsed his race for the Illinois state senate. The DSA bills itself as the largest socialist organization in America and the principal U.S. affiliate of the Socialist International. Nor should we ignore that Obama campaigned for self-identified socialist senator Bernie Sanders of Vermont. In 2007, the *National Journal* dubbed Obama the most liberal member of the United States Senate— ahead of even Sanders.[52]

Obama racked up quite a liberal record in the Illinois Senate as well. He cut his teeth there on socialized medicine advocacy for the state, but he was always able to use his personal charisma to blunt the perception that he was an extremist.

But it's been suggested that one of Obama's voluntary relationships is more revealing of his radicalism, anti-Americanism, and anti-capitalism than all of the others: his choice of marital partner. The columnist known as Spengler, writing for the *Asia Times,* quoted Alexandre Dumas: "When you want to uncover an unspecified secret, look for the woman." In Obama's case, wrote Spengler, there have been two principal women in his life: his late mother and "his rancorous wife Michelle. Obama's women reveal his secret: he hates America."[53]

As everyone knows, Michelle Obama caused a stir when she commented, in a speech, that "for the first time in my adult lifetime, I am really proud of my country."[54] At the time, her defenders were quick to dismiss the comment as an unfortunate extemporaneous remark—until video surfaced that confirmed she'd made exactly the same statement in another speech. And, as Spengler noted, the sentiment wasn't new to her: It was the theme of her undergraduate thesis on "blackness" at Princeton.

Spengler's conclusion was that the influences that created the "real Barack Obama" were not just his political or spiritual advisers, but the women with whom he had spent his life. "No man—least of all one abandoned in infancy by his father—can conceal the imprint of an impassioned mother, or the influence of a brilliant wife."

But Ann Dunham and Michelle Obama would have stiff competition for the title of chief influence over Barack Obama. His adult life has been riddled with troubling associations, which together offer a kind of capsule portrait of a young radical in training.

TWO

OBAMA'S NEW RADICAL FRIENDS

Obama's ever-diminishing ranks of defenders would have more credibility in denying the relevance of the president's radical past if it weren't for his record of appointing extremist after extremist to various executive positions and judgeships. We're all known by the company we keep, and Obama consistently—and deliberately—keeps company with hard leftists. If the mainstream media weren't in the tank for Obama, if they disclosed the extent of his connections with radicals and the extent of these radicals' extremism, the nation would be in a greater uproar than it already is.

In addition to media cover, Obama has another thing going for him: The truth about him and his inner circle is stranger than fiction. He couldn't be more of a Manchurian candidate if he were auditioning for the role in the movie. This stuff is just too bizarre for most Americans to process: an actual Marxist in the White House who has surrounded himself with like-minded miscreants.

Let's just take a mini-survey of his foxhole comrades.

MARILYN KATZ

Some might think it unfair to paint Obama as a leftist radical simply on the strength of the views of his political allies; his defenders might say he has little control over his supporters or what kind of people they are. Fair enough, to a point—though it's hardly meaningless that the Communist Party of the United States of America endorsed Obama for president,[1] or that its national chair hailed Obama's victory as "a repudiation of right-wing ideology, politics and economics and a setback for neo-liberalism in both its conservative and liberal skins." By the same token, the fact that Obama's campaign organization has included figures like Marilyn Katz is no insignificant detail: It's a clear indication of the kinds of people he's comfortable having carry his flag.

Katz has an unmistakably radical past, one that includes advocating guerilla tactics during the Chicago Democratic Convention riots of 1968. During the famous Chicago Seven trial the following year, undercover policeman William Frapolly testified that, one night in the city's Lincoln Park, Katz briefed a group of protesters on a new addition to their arsenal of anarchy: guerrilla nails—nails that were sharpened at both ends and used for throwing or putting underneath tires.[2] Katz was reportedly head of security for the hard-core leftist group Students for a Democratic Society (SDS). It's shocking to realize that this woman who once engaged in such an insurrection against law and order went on to become one of Barack Obama's key campaign organizers.[3]

Katz didn't go on to become part of the "bombs and bullets approach of Ayers, Inc.," as one columnist put it, but she certainly continued her work as a leftist activist. She was one of the principal organizers of Obama's 2002 antiwar rally where he warned against the liberation of Iraq. The Obama campaign has embraced Katz, putting her on its national finance committee and listing her as a "bundler" on Obama's website. She has hosted fund-raisers for Obama, contributed thousands to his campaign, and serves as a member of the credentials committee for the Illinois delegation to the Democratic National Convention.[4]

Marilyn Katz, then, was there at the start of Obama's bid for the White House. But her involvement is just the tip of the iceberg. Obama's inner circle is full of advisers with lifelong leftist pedigrees.

DAVID AXELROD

David Axelrod is probably Obama's chief adviser—his close friend and political guru, the man who feeds his teleprompter, the man who's got his back. The significance of his role cannot be overstated. In his *New York Times* profile of Axelrod, Jeff Zeleny wrote, "His title does little to capture his full importance to Mr. Obama. His voice, and political advice, carries more weight than most anyone else's on the president's payroll. . . . There are few words that come across the president's lips that have not been blessed by Mr. Axelrod. He reviews every speech, studies every major policy position and works with Robert Gibbs, the White House press secretary, to prepare responses to the crisis of the day."[5]

Not surprisingly, Axelrod, like Obama, received mentoring from leftist radicals in Chicago. The *Chicago Tribune* reported that Axelrod's mentor was Don Rose, a political strategist who "carved out a reputation for himself as a skillful specialist working for local progressive candidates."[6] Along with David Canter, a leftist political activist, Rose owned the *Hyde Park–Kenwood Voices,* a small newspaper with a radical slant, which took on such causes as launching a campaign to abolish the House Committee on Un-American Activities. The paper sympathetically reported the SDS riots at the 1968 Democratic Convention in Chicago.[7] According to David Canter's son, Marc Canter, Don Rose remembers that Axelrod's political curiosity was nurtured by Canter and Rose. In an email Marc posted on his website, he confirmed that "your dad [David Canter] and I 'mentored' and helped educate [Axelrod] politically" when Axelrod was a young man.[8]

VALERIE JARRETT

Valerie Jarrett is a senior adviser for Obama, and, perhaps not coincidentally, a close personal friend of Marilyn Katz.[9] Where Karl Rove was tagged as George W. Bush's "brain," Jarrett is known as "the other side of Barack Obama's brain," and as his "eyes and ears." She has been described as "the most powerful woman in Chicago besides Oprah," an adviser who has "earned the complete confidence of Barack and Michelle Obama."[10] A *New York Times* profile describes her as the person to see if you need to persuade Obama of the wisdom of any given course of action. When others can't get through to him, there are two who can: Michelle Obama and Valerie Jarrett. She is the one person in the White House who "gets the boss," in much the same way Karen Hughes "got" George W. Bush, Bruce Lindsey "got" Bill Clinton, and Jim Baker "got" the first President Bush. Obama himself has described Jarrett as "someone I trust completely. She is family." Obama trusts her "to speak for me, particularly when we're dealing with delicate issues."[11]

The president's "alter ego" was instrumental in recruiting and choosing the radical (and now disgraced) Van Jones to serve as green energy czar. To an audience at the Daily Kos blogger conference, she bragged about "all the creative ideas [Jones] has. And so now . . . we have all that energy and enthusiasm in the White House."[12]

As the *Chicago Tribune* reported, before coming to the White House Jarrett headed up the Habitat Company, a real estate corporation that managed a number of sizable housing projects in the Chicago area.[13] Habitat received federal and state subsidies for two of its projects, Grove Parc Plaza and Lawndale Restoration, but as the *American Spectator* reported, they "were ultimately seized by federal authorities for what were unlivable conditions."[14] During her time at Habitat, Jarrett also worked with Obama pal Tony Rezko, a convicted felon, raising campaign funds for the young candidate.[15]

Jarrett is said to be serving as Obama's conduit for far-leftists into the administration. She is another insider obsessed with racial issues. She was behind the push to relax restrictions on officials meeting with lobbyists—contradicting an explicit Obama campaign promise and executive memo.[16] Jarrett was behind the creation of the position of "diversity czar," the chief diversity officer of the Federal Communications Commission, and the recruitment of law professor Cass Sunstein for regulatory czar.

MARK LLOYD

At the behest of Valerie Jarrett, our ostensibly "postracial" president created the position of diversity czar. And how did he choose to fill it? With one Mark Lloyd, whom NewsBusters.org describes as "virulently anti-capitalist, almost myopically racially fixated and exuberantly pro-regulation," not to mention— surprise!—another "Saul Alinsky disciple."[17] Lloyd once served as a senior fellow at the far-left Center for American Progress, where he coauthored a chilling report in 2007, "The Structural Imbalance of Political Talk Radio," which offers "remedies" to undermine conservative talk and bolster liberal talk.

Lloyd is also the author of *Prologue to a Farce: Communication and Democracy in America*, a 2006 book in which he advocates a "confrontational movement" against private media. His goal? To marshal leftist activists to exert political pressure on politicians to impose confiscatory fees, fines, and regulations to drive commercial broadcasters out, to be replaced by public broadcasters. Like a true leftist, Lloyd doesn't approach constitutional rights neutrally, but rather from a class perspective. The freedoms of speech and press, he says, are "all too often an exaggeration. At the very least, blind references to freedom of speech or the press serve as a distraction from the critical examination of other communications policies. The purpose of free speech is warped to protect global corporations and block rules that would promote democratic governance." Viewing these sacred First Amendment freedoms more as weapons for the power elites, Lloyd probably has little incentive to safeguard their sanctity. Lloyd's bizarre perspective on free speech as a weapon will probably serve as one of the many rationalizations Obama and his leftist censors plan on invoking when they start trying to selectively enforce free speech protections, using the Fairness Doctrine, local diversity rules, and the like—precisely what they've falsely accused others of doing.

One of the left's favorite tactics is the Orwellian distortion of language, including the use of euphemisms, to disguise their unpopular beliefs and policies to make them more palatable to the electorate. They use "progressive" instead of "liberal," knowing the latter has come to mean high taxes, softness on crime, appeasement of our enemies, and secularism. They use "community organizing" to mask the true activity of the political agitator. They use "economic justice" in place of "redistribution of wealth." They sometimes use "working folks" to describe those who don't pay any taxes at all. They use "investments" for "government spending." They call taxes "contributions," and refer to pro-abortion groups as "pro-choice" advocates fighting for "reproductive rights." They call forced union membership "free choice." And they use the cloak of the so-called "Fairness Doctrine" to conceal their sinister plan to unfairly stack the playing field against conservative talk radio.

In that spirit of turning words and concepts on their heads, Mark Lloyd contends that the free speech laws in place today need to be changed because they block democratic governance. Yet the rules *he* wants to impose would do precisely that—impede democracy—via the Fairness Doctrine and its evil cousins.

Just look at how Lloyd has twisted the very word *democracy* in analyzing events in Venezuela. In describing the Venezuelan dictator and thug Hugo Chavez, for example, he says: "In Venezuela, with Chavez," there is

> really an incredible revolution—a democratic revolution. To
> begin to put in place things that are going to have an impact

on the people of Venezuela. The property owners and the folks who then controlled the media in Venezuela rebelled—worked, frankly, with folks here in the U.S. government—worked to oust him. But he came back with another revolution, and then Chavez began to take very seriously the media in his country. And we've had complaints about this ever since.

Who were these property owners Lloyd was vilifying? They were *the victims of Chavez's repressive regime.* Chavez was stealing their property and nationalizing their industries. Yet Lloyd's sympathy was with this thug and not his victims.[18] It's that kind of tainted perspective that makes so many of us concerned, in turn, about the perspective of the man who appointed him: Barack Obama.

But what's even more ominous about Lloyd's statement is his comment about Chavez taking the media "seriously." How exactly did he take the media seriously? Well, let's see: Legislators who are loyal to Chavez drafted legislation that could "financially strangle" his critics; imposed new regulations on cable television; revoked the licenses of 240 radio stations; and attempted to seize control of certain media to suppress their criticism.[19] And a government prosecutor, General Luisa Ortega, proposed a Media Crimes bill that would expand the government's ability to punish media critics for actions or omissions it found objectionable.[20]

These are the kinds of positive steps our new diversity czar applauds in Chavez's so-called "democratic revolution."

CASS SUNSTEIN

And Mark Lloyd isn't the only Obama czar with radical views. Cass Sunstein, his "regulatory czar," takes a very unorthodox view of one of our nation's most precious principles: the First Amendment's guarantee of free speech. As Kyle Smith wrote in the *New York Post,* Sunstein believes the courts should be used to impose a "chilling effect" on speech that might hurt someone's feelings, and that new laws need to be written to regulate it.[21]

Sunstein subscribes to a philosophy he calls "libertarian paternalism," which supports private and public institutions "steering people's choices in welfare-promoting directions without eliminating freedom of choice." I suppose this is on par with Obama's bizarre contention that his public option for health care was designed to increase consumer choice, rather than create a wholesale government monopoly over the health care industry.

Sunstein believes that animals, through human beings, should be able to bring private lawsuits to ensure that anticruelty and related laws are actually enforced.[22] In the introduction to a book called *Animal Rights: Current Debates and New Directions*, Sunstein suggested that animal rights should be considered comparable with civil rights, abortion rights, and gay marriage rights.[23]

Sunstein's compassion for animals apparently doesn't quite extend to the unborn: He reportedly holds strong pro-abortion and pro-human-cloning views. In 2003 he wrote, "If scientists will be using and cloning embryos only at a very early stage when they are just a handful of cells (say, before they are four days old), there is no good reason for a ban. It is silly to think that 'potential' is enough for moral concern. Sperm cells have 'potential' and (not to put too fine a point on it) most people are not especially solicitous about them."[24] An analysis by Phyllis Schlafly's Eagle Forum concluded that Sunstein regards euthanasia as a major component of health-care legislation. Sunstein would apply a cost-benefit analysis when making health care decisions for the elderly. According to the Eagle Forum, "Sunstein's views on cost-effectiveness analysis [are] worrisome at best, especially since as head of the Office of Information and Regulatory Affairs, he will play a major role in defining the government's handling of health care."[25]

RON BLOOM

None of Obama's appointments has been more shocking to the freedom lover's conscience than his selection of Ron Bloom on September 7, 2009, as "manufacturing czar." Obviously believing that creating jobs—and specifically targeted ones such as manufacturing jobs—is primarily the responsibility of government, not the private sector, Obama appointed Bloom to "help us craft policies that will create the next generation of great manufacturing jobs and ensure American competitiveness in the 21st century." Bloom has strong labor union ties, having begun as a high-powered negotiator for the notorious SEIU and served as a special assistant to the president of the United Steelworkers.[26] Only a chief executive as soft on unions as Obama is could think it's a good idea to hire a labor union negotiator to help create manufacturing jobs.

But it's not just Bloom's résumé that should concern Americans. It's his radical beliefs, which he hasn't been shy about sharing. At the sixth annual Distressed Investing Forum at the Union League Club in New York on February 27–28, 2008, Bloom made some shocking comments. The "free market is nonsense," he declared; "the whole point is to game the system." Bloom said that he and his colleagues recognize that "this is largely about power"—and, shockingly, that "we kind of agree with Mao [Zedong] that political power comes largely from the barrel of a gun." That's right, Obama's manufacturing czar kind-of agrees with Red China's Chairman Mao, the tyrant responsible for murdering tens of millions of his own people during peacetime for not toeing the party line. How comforting is that?

ANITA DUNN

And the same wonderful Chinese dictator has entranced another of Obama's radical darlings—Obama's short-lived White House communications director Anita Dunn, who regards Mao as among her favorite philosophers. Obama is nothing if not consistent. Dunn fit in quite well with Obama's diversity czar, Mark Lloyd; her war on Fox News would have made Hugo Chavez proud.[27] During her tenure at the White House, Dunn barked that Fox was "opinion journalism masquerading as news," sneering, "Let's not pretend they're a news network the way CNN is." Fox, she said, "operates almost as either the research arm or the communications arm of the Republican Party." Interesting, but I never got the memo. It might be more accurate to say that Obama had something against Fox: After all, Fox has continually invited Obama on its programs to air his views, but he has repeatedly declined. On September 20, 2009, when he appeared on five other Sunday shows, he defiantly refused to accept an invitation to appear with Chris Wallace on *Fox News Sunday*.

After the White House started taking heat for its attack on Fox—for which Dunn, of course, was just the messenger—Obama canned her, saying that her position had been temporary all along. I find it fascinating that the White House cashiered Dunn after she did the same thing that President Obama has done to me personally (not that I'm complaining): On my radio show, I play an audio montage that lasts more than a minute of Obama calling me out by name, complaining about my unfavorable treatment of him, and suggesting, at one point, that one of his fans engage in debate with me and "tear me up." The White House has even stooped to using its government blog—which should be *the people's blog*—to slander this network for what it calls "Fox lies."

VAN JONES

Obama outdid himself with the appointment of Van Jones as "green czar"—a decision he had to reverse when Jones's radicalism came to light. Of course, this didn't happen right away: Obama's minions first defended the appointment, complaining that Jones was being attacked by the extreme right. When that strategy failed, they backed off, grumbling only that the White House hadn't properly vetted Jones. As if Jones's beliefs weren't perfectly in tune with those of Obama's radical troupe!

Of all the Obama clan's views, Jones's may have been the most outrageous. In 2004 he signed a petition calling for an investigation to determine whether government officials allowed the 9/11 terrorist attacks to happen, or were even behind them. He supported the convicted cop killer Mumia Abu-Jamal. In 2008 he accused "white polluters" of "steering poison into the people of color communities." And at a speech in Berkeley, California, he called Republicans "a—holes"[28]—a comment that probably earned him the appointment in the first place.

But Jones wasn't just some kind of hothead or conspiracy

nut: Throughout much of the 1990s, he was a self-identified communist. The *East Bay Express* quoted Jones as saying that when he was jailed during the Rodney King riots in Los Angeles in 1992, "I met all these young radical people of color—I mean really radical, communists and anarchists. And it was like, this is what I need to be a part of. . . . I spent the next ten years of my life working with a lot of those people I met in jail, trying to be a revolutionary. . . . I was a rowdy nationalist on April 28th, and then the verdicts came down on April 29th. By August, I was a communist." In the same interview, Jones said that his environmental activism was a vehicle to fight for racial and class justice. "Our question is," he said, "will the green wave lift all boats? That's the moral challenge to the people who are the architects of this new, ecologically sound economy. Will we have eco-equity, or will we have eco-apartheid? Right now we have eco-apartheid."[29] Echoes of Reverend Wright, anyone?

KEVIN JENNINGS

Then there's Obama's "safe schools czar," longtime homosexual activist Kevin Jennings. Jennings has a history of statements and associations that are troubling for anyone appointed to oversee the American educational system.

As Jennings has written in his memoirs, as a young gay man he violently and blasphemously rejected his Christian upbringing. "Before, I was the one who was failing God; now I decided He was the one who had failed me. . . . I decided I had done nothing wrong: *He* had, by promising to 'set you free' and never delivering on His promise. What *had* He done for me, other than make me feel shame and guilt? Squat. Screw you, buddy—I don't need you around anymore, I decided." He retained his hatred toward religious leaders into adulthood: At a meeting with fellow activists in 2000, he condemned the "religious right" as "hard-core bigots" who should "drop dead," and declared that he really wanted to tell them, "F— you!"

But Jennings's feelings toward national and religious institutions go beyond the personal; they have also colored his professional life. He was on the advisory board for a PBS documentary that attacked the Boy Scouts of America for excluding homosexuals from membership—a video that has been used at gay pride conventions to motivate activists to work against the Scouts.

He has also been strongly criticized for introducing homosexual themes into public schools (including elementary schools), for writing the foreword for a book called *Queering Elementary Education*, and for his association with the homosexual activist group Gay, Lesbian, and Straight Education Network (GLSEN).[30] The chapters of *Queering Elementary Education* include "Teaching Queerly: Some Elementary Propositions," "Why Discuss Sexuality in Elementary School?" and "Locating a Place for Gay and Lesbian Themes in Elementary Reading, Writing, and Talking."

To give you an idea of the mentality of GLSEN, which Jennings founded, one report on the Gateway Pundit blog offers a detailed account of the XXX-rated reading list the organization recommends for children—complete with extensive, sexually explicit quotations from many of the books. The site quotes a report from Breitbart.tv that "book after book after book contained stories and anecdotes that weren't merely X-rated and pornographic, but which featured explicit descriptions of sex acts between preschoolers; stories that seemed to promote and recommend child-adult sexual relationships; stories of public masturbation, anal sex in restrooms, affairs between students and teachers, five-year-olds playing sex games, semen flying through the air."[31]

Representative Steve King (R-Iowa) has called on Obama to fire Jennings, saying that "the totality of his life has been the promotion of homosexuality, and much of it within education. He has focused on nothing else during the last two decades, and that is not the focus that our schools need to be on."[32]

Those who insist the White House doesn't vet these radicals should take into account White House Press Secretary Robert Gibbs's unflinching defense of Jennings *after* reports of his homosexual radicalism surfaced. When asked whether Obama was standing by Jennings, Gibbs referred the press to a statement from Secretary of Education Arne Duncan, a big Jennings supporter. The statement said, "Kevin Jennings has dedicated his professional career to promoting school safety. He is uniquely qualified for his job and I'm honored to have him on our team."[33] Uniquely qualified to serve in *this* administration, to be sure.

HARRY KNOX

Along these same lines, Obama appointed Harry Knox to his Advisory Council on Faith-Based and Neighborhood Partnerships. Knox is a militant homosexual activist who called Pope Benedict XVI and certain Catholic bishops "discredited leaders" because they opposed same-sex marriage. He castigated the Knights of Columbus as "foot soldiers of a discredited army of oppression" for supporting California's Proposition 8 ballot initiative to amend the state constitution to define marriage as between a man and a woman. When challenged, he would not back down on his criticism of the pope, saying "the Pope needs to start telling the truth about condom use." Knox even condemned the teachings of the apostle Paul as "not true." "Paul," he said, "did not have any idea of the kind of love that I feel for a partner when I am partnered. . . . The straight man, the heterosexual man, Paul, didn't think it was natural because for him it must not have been."[34]

CAROL BROWNER

In January 2009, Obama appointed Carol M. Browner as his "global warming czar." The *Washington Examiner* has unabashedly called Browner an environmental radical and a socialist. "There is no question about the socialism," the paper writes. "By appointing Browner to a White House post, Obama has at least implicitly endorsed an utterly radical socialist agenda for his administration's environmental policy."[35] Before the appointment, Browner had been listed as one of fourteen leaders of the Commission for a Sustainable World Society, which calls for "global governance" and says that rich countries must shrink their economies to address climate change. Is it any wonder that Obama's policies are necessarily shrinking our economy—not to mention bankrupting us?

The commission is the action arm on climate change for Socialist International, an umbrella group for many of the world's social democratic political parties that is very critical of U.S. policies. Again, Obama makes no apologies for this appointment; he knew exactly what he was getting with Browner, as his subsequent policies on global warming have confirmed. When challenged on Browner's membership on the commission,

Obama's transition team said it was not a problem—indeed, that it would even add experience in U.S. policy making to her new role.

If you still have lingering doubts about Browner's dubious environmental credentials, one more thing to consider: She also served on the board of directors for Al Gore's Alliance for Climate Protection.[36]

JOHN HOLDREN

Obama's director of the Office of Science and Technology Policy (OSTP), or "science czar," is John Holdren, another leftist with beliefs outside the American mainstream. In his writings, Holdren seems to approve of and recommend compulsory sterilization and even sometimes abortion, in furtherance of a government population control program.

In 1977, Holdren cowrote (with Paul and Anne Ehrlich) a book called *Ecoscience*—a volume that sounds a disturbingly casual note concerning the prospect of compulsory population control. "Several coercive proposals deserve discussion, mainly because some countries may ultimately have to resort to them unless current trends in birth rates are rapidly reversed by other means," the authors wrote. "Some involuntary measures could be less repressive or discriminatory, in fact, than some of the socioeconomic measures suggested." The authors defended the Indian government's move toward implementing a compulsory sterilization program in the mid-1970s. They wrote, "This decision was greeted with dismay abroad, but Indira Gandhi's government felt it had little other choice. There is too little time left to experiment further with educational programs and hope that social change will generate a spontaneous fertility decline, and most of the Indian population is too poor for direct economic pressures (especially penalties) to be effective."

Most shocking, though, was the authors' purely utilitarian analysis of proposals to put sterilants into the drinking water or staple foods of a population. The authors do not recommend such an approach, but, as author David Freddoso observes, the objections they express have more to do with practical and health considerations than any moral reservations or concerns for human freedom. "Adding a sterilant to drinking water or staple foods is a suggestion that seems to horrify people more than most proposals for involuntary fertility control," they write. "Indeed, this would pose some very difficult political, legal, and social questions, to say nothing of the technical problems." Where is the moral outrage? Later in the paragraph, they add: "And the risk of serious, unforeseen side effects would, in our opinion militate against the use of any such agent, even though this plan has the advantage of avoiding the need for socioeconomic pressures that might tend to discriminate against particular groups or penalize children."[37]

Michelle Malkin, a Fox News contributor, reports that she called Holdren's White House office "to press Science Czar John Holdren on his views; his purported disavowal of *Ecoscience* . . . and his continued embrace of forced-abortion advocate and eugenics guru Harrison Brown, whom he credits with inspiring him to become a scientist," but that she was stonewalled. "When I pressed [OSTP staffer Rick Weiss] specifically about Holdren's relationship with Harrison Brown, he: 1) said he didn't know who he was; 2) balked at drawing any conclusions about Holdren's views based on his homages to Brown (even though Brown is a lifelong intellectual mentor, colleague, and continued inspiration for Holdren); 3) and told me not to expect any response from

Holdren's office on my specific question about whether Holdren disavows his relationship with a eugenics enthusiast who referred to the world population as a 'pulsating mass of maggots.'"[38]

KATHLEEN SEBELIUS

Obama chose Kathleen Sebelius to be his Health and Human Services secretary, a choice that riled pro-life groups and especially Catholics—because, with her unusual status as both a self-identified Catholic and an abortion supporter, Sebelius's advocacy is divisive. As Catholic League president Bill Donahue said, "Catholics do not expect abortion-rights presidents will go out of their way to choose pro-life Catholics to be in their administration. But they also don't expect them to go out of their way to offend them. Obama has done just that."[39] Archbishop Joseph Naumann of Kansas City, Kansas, asked Sebelius to refrain from receiving Holy Communion, saying that her abortion position had "grave spiritual and moral consequences."[40] Sebelius's views on abortion are so far to the left that she even supports late-term abortions—much like Obama himself. She fought as an elected official in Kansas against popular, but relatively modest pro-life measures such as parental consent and efforts to curb late-term abortions. Sebelius also enjoyed a close personal and financial relationship with the infamous Dr. George Tiller, who specialized in late-term abortions and confessed to having performed some sixty thousand abortions.[41]

HAROLD KOH

Obama's appointment mischief doesn't stop with his "czar" picks; it extends to judges and public officials of all sorts. He appointed former Yale Law School dean Harold Koh as legal adviser for the State Department. In his position, Koh represents the United States before international bodies such as the United Nations and the International Court of Justice, and has a role in just how far other countries' laws will influence the American legal system.

A mere cursory review of Koh's writings and speeches reveals that he favors—to an alarming degree—the practice of liberal judges of considering laws of other nations in their interpretation of our constitution. In a piece for the *Fordham Law Review,* Koh, who is a transnationalist, explained the differences between transnationalists and nationalists, both of whom serve on the Supreme Court. Transnationalists, he said, think about how U.S. law fits into a framework of transnational law and believe that courts can "domesticate" international law—that is, make it part of our law. Nationalists believe that only the political branches have the constitutional authority to do that. The Constitution isn't a great hurdle for Koh and his like-minded transnationalists because they believe in an ever-changing, living Constitution. They are not so hung up on arcane conservative concepts like national sovereignty, believing that there is an international "community of reason" (foreign laws) that can inform American jurisprudence.

Koh shares with his ultimate boss, President Obama, a disdain for America's pre-Obama behavior. He actually said that the United States, along with North Korea and Iran, formed "the axis of disobedience"—whose "disobedience with international law has attracted global attention after Sept. 11." In Koh's Senate Judiciary Committee testimony of September 16, 2008, he said that the United States had forfeited the "universal sympathy" she enjoyed as a victim of the 9/11 attacks with a "series of self-inflicted wounds, which have gravely diminished our global standing and damaged our reputation for respecting the rule of law"[42]—sentiments that could have come straight from Obama's mouth.

Equally troubling is Koh's attitude toward the application of Muslim sharia law in American courts. In a 2007 speech to the Yale Club of Greenwich, Connecticut, he said that "in an appropriate case, he didn't see any reason why sharia law would not be applied to govern a case in the United States."

DAWN JOHNSEN

Obama appointed Dawn Johnsen to head the Justice Department's Office of Legal Counsel despite her radical views—including that pregnancy can be comparable to involuntary servitude.[43] In addition, according to Andrew McCarthy of *National Review*, Johnsen rejects all of the traditional, widely accepted, commonsense impediments to abortion: "She opposes 24-hour waiting periods, parental-consent requirements for minors, and laws against partial-birth abortion." Similarly disturbing is her infernal laxity regarding our national security. Not only does she oppose the George W. Bush administration's handling of the war on terror; she wrote that the Obama administration "should order an immediate review to determine which detainees should be released and which transferred to secure facilities in the United States."[44]

OTHERS

- Obama's first appellate court appointee was radical pro-abortion judge **DAVID HAMILTON**, who, as a district judge in Indiana, issued rulings over seven years that prevented Indiana from implementing its informed-consent law, which was designed to give pregnant women important information about the risks and alternatives to abortion.[45]

• Obama appointed **ROSA BROOKS** as adviser to the undersecretary of defense for policy, one of the most influential positions in the Pentagon. In 2007, Brooks referred to Al Qaeda as "little more than an obscure group of extremist thugs, well financed and intermittently lethal but relatively limited in their global and regional political pull." Brooks's view of the terrorist network was both offensive and dangerously cavalier: "On 9/11, they got lucky," she wrote. "Thanks to U.S. policies, al-Qaida has become the vast global threat the administration imagined it to be in 2001."[46] No, to Brooks, the real threats were—you guessed it!—President Bush and Vice President Dick Cheney, who "should be treated like psychotics who need treatment," in her view. "Impeachment's not the solution to psychosis, no matter how flagrant."[47]

• Another dubious Obama associate is **JODIE EVANS**, who was a cofounder of the antiwar organization Code Pink— a group best known for its disruptive protests of congressional sessions. During the campaign she was a fund-raising bundler for Obama and helped raise at least fifty thousand dollars for his campaign. According to Politico, she is an activist liberal who has worked in liberal causes for decades. GOP sources reported that Evans has a record of inflammatory statements—contending that Iraqi women were better off under Saddam Hussein;

that "men are dying in their Hummers in Iraq so you can drive around in yours"; and that Bush's attack on Iraq was a matter of "global testosterone poisoning." [48]

Evans reportedly met with the Taliban in Afghanistan on a recent trip there. [49] She was captured on videotape a few weeks later handing a package to Obama in a receiving line at a fund-raiser in San Francisco; it contained a petition supporting the women of Afghanistan against a troop surge there. In one interview Evans praised the Taliban for bringing peace and justice to Afghanistan, and said that America had failed to deliver either. In another interview Evans said the United States had created a "hell on earth" in Afghanistan. [50] Interestingly, BigGovernment.com later reported that White House logs showed that Evans met with Buffy Wicks, the deputy director of the White House Office of Public Engagement, on June 19, 2009, just days after Code Pink visited Hamas in Gaza and accepted a letter to deliver to Obama. [51]

- One of Obama's key foreign policy advisers, from the beginning, has been Cass Sunstein's wife, SAMANTHA POWER, a writer and academic. As *The American Thinker*'s Richard Baehr and Ed Lasky warned in 2008, Power's presence on the Obama team would not be comforting to supporters of Israel. Power, they wrote, "seems obsessed with Israel, and in a negative way. . . . Her approach to addressing the Israeli-Palestinian conflict would be for the US to . . . withdraw support for Israel, and instead apply more pressure on Israel for concessions." [52]

At the notoriously Israel-bashing World Conference

Against Racism in 2001, Power said that regardless of the danger of "alienating" Jewish Americans, "a domestic constituency of tremendous political and financial import," the United States should take the "billions of dollars" it had spent "servicing Israel's military" and invest it instead in "the new state of Palestine."[53] On the topic of Iran, Power also calls for the United States to "engage diplomatically the mullahs and pretend the Iranian nuclear program is a figment of the paranoid imagination of the Bush administration."[54]

Though Power resigned from Obama's 2008 campaign after calling Hillary Clinton "a monster," she later came aboard Obama's transition team, working for the State Department. In January 2009, Obama appointed her to the National Security Council, as director for multilateral affairs.

The number of czars—or those with czarlike powers—on Obama's team varies, but most place it conservatively in excess of thirty. In addition to those already mentioned, there's Afghanistan czar Richard Holbrooke, auto recovery czar Ed Montgomery, border czar Alan Bersin, California water czar David Hayes, Central Region czar Dennis Ross, domestic violence czar Lynn Rosenthal, drug czar Gil Kerlikowske, faith-based czar Joshua DuBois, Great Lakes czar Cameron Davis, Guantanamo closure czar Daniel Fried, health czar Nancy-Ann DeParle, information czar Vivek Kundra, international climate czar Todd Stern, intelligence czar Dennis Blair, Mideast peace czar George Mitchell, pay czar Kenneth Feinberg, stimulus accountability czar Earl Devaney, Sudan czar J. Scott Gration, TARP czar Herb Allison, terrorism czar John Brennan, technology czar Aneesh Chopra, urban affairs czar Adolfo Carrion, Jr., weapons czar Ashton Carter, and WMD policy czar Gary Samore.

What's truly alarming, beyond the radical nature of most of these Obama czars, is what such a proliferation of advisers—especially those not under the regulatory purview of Congress—says about Obama's vision of the expanding powers of the federal government. Do you think the framers could have imagined an urban affairs czar? Not *everything* is the business of the federal government—no matter how much liberals want to control every aspect of our lives.

When liberals ceaselessly complained about President George W. Bush's executive power grabs, some of us recognized that this was just another case of liberal projection. If the Democrats were to retake control of the executive branch, we could see the explosion of new executive powers coming a mile away. So none of this should come as any surprise. But it's not just a matter of the executive branch growing. It's that this particular manner of expansion—through unaccountable czars—interferes with the separation of powers and the proper balance between the three branches of the federal government. In many cases, these czars are more important than official, accountable presidential cabinet members. Obama is deliberately shifting power to this cadre of unaccountables.

But liberals aren't about to allow a little trifle like the Constitution's prescribed structure of government to interfere with their utopian vision for America—the latest iteration of which is Obama's mission to fundamentally remake America in his image. Just as they contort the First Amendment to protect only their pet causes and people, the Constitution's provisions for legislative oversight of certain executive offices and functions must be conveniently ignored when liberal political expedience so dictates. But with Congress under the firm control of Obama's Democrats as well, don't hold your breath waiting for the legislative branch to reassert itself and rein in Obama's executive branch.

Congress, under Obama's Democrats, is not just passively ceding its power to the executive branch in areas it shouldn't. In concert with Obama, it too is stealing power from the people. Congressmen are deliberately ignoring their own rules (such as Al Franken cutting off Republican senators speaking in opposition to Obama's agenda); they're voting on legislation when not only have they not read it, but it hasn't even been written; they're spending trillions of dollars we don't have and can't possibly acquire; they're allocating monies to corrupt groups like ACORN to ensure their own reelection rather than for any legitimate legislative purpose; and they're doing all this in defiance of the will of the people.

This from the group that cynically promised a new era of transparency in government.

But among the Democrats' many shameless attempts to seize power away from the people, the granddaddy of them all is contained in the Senate health-care bill. Unbeknownst to many, that bill contains an amendment, inserted by Majority Leader Harry Reid, that aims to make the bill's proposed Independent Medicare Advisory Board (IMAB) unrepealable. The amendment would change certain Senate rules to prohibit future Congresses from repealing the IMAB (which some refer to as a death panel). But current Senate rules require sixty-seven votes for a rule change. The Democrats, who had already changed the rule with their sixty-vote (not sixty-seven-vote) majority, claimed they weren't changing the rule, just changing a "procedure." But their intentions were clear: Obama's Senate was not only trying to make their provision for death panels unrepealable—violating our first principles of popular sovereignty at their core—but in the process they were also violating their own rules through semantic deception. As Fox News contributor William Kristol wrote in the *Weekly Standard*, "The heart of the bill is the attempt to get control of our health care permanently in the hands of the federal bureaucrats, who would allegedly know better than doctors and patients what's good for them, and who would cut access to care and the quality of care so there's more money left over for various big government liberal social programs."[55] And yet the Democrats still feign outrage at the *suggestion* that they support health-care rationing—particularly for the elderly.

CONNECTING THE DOTS: RADICAL CONNECTIONS TO POLICY AGENDA

During the 2008 campaign, it wasn't just the liberal media or the Democratic Party apparatus telling us Barack Obama was a moderate man with congenial propensities, a paragon of bipartisanship who would make the perfect postracial president. A number of pseudoconservatives were singing from the same hymnbook. But some of us saw from the start that Obama was a radical's radical, and we sounded the warning bell early. The destructiveness of Obama's policy agenda was as predictable as it was horrifying. Obama's past radical associations were not a matter of happenstance. They were a logical result of the way he was raised, mentored, and indoctrinated. His radical appointments and policies today are entirely consistent with the radical associations of his past, and they are a harbinger of his radical agenda for the future.

That's the most important thing to understand about the Obama administration.

I don't highlight the radical résumé of Obama's brain trust for the purpose of demonizing the man—though that's an inevitable by-product of the facts. The point is to demonstrate who the real Barack Obama is. He is a radical organizing his fellow radicals. He is the agitator who has deliberately created an environment of panic and hysteria in order to rush through extraordinarily overreaching legislation that is designed to control every aspect of our lives. He is the indefatigable perpetual motion machine hell-bent on obliterating our free market system in favor of a command-control economy and political system.

As we briefly survey his domestic and foreign policy agendas in the next two chapters, we'll see that they too are products of the radical ideology he has been honing his entire life. With Obama, nothing is a coincidence. He knows precisely what he's doing and where he's going, and he doesn't intend to allow anything—including the unequivocal opposition of an over-whelming majority of the American people—to get in his way.

We ignore this at our nation's peril.

THREE

OBAMA THE SOCIALIST

I suppose that the powerful influence of Marxist parents and mentors is just too much for certain people to resist. It would be nice—or at least honest—if Barack Obama would just come out and admit his socialism. Then again, if he had done so before the election, he'd never have received more than 30 percent of the vote in this center-right nation, even during very difficult economic times.

But as much as Obama tried to conceal his radical ideology, he didn't always succeed. His smug retort to Joe the Plumber about spreading the wealth around was just the tip of the iceberg. He did let America know, in no uncertain terms, that he wanted universal health care—which is a euphemism for socialized medicine. He made it clear, in his language and ideas, that he sees the world in Marxist, class-warfare terms. He blamed America's economic problems on capitalists and capitalism, on big business, Wall Street, insurance companies, oil companies, and the wealthy.

Ever since Bill and Hillary Clinton brought their mantra against "trickle-down economics" to Washington, Democrats have demagogued the issue of tax cuts, always saying that "the wealthy" haven't paid their fair share of taxes. That's about the best they could do in their feeble effort to undermine the enormous empirical successes of the Reagan and Bush tax cuts. The claim is completely specious. In the first place, under the Bush tax cuts, higher income earners paid a higher percentage marginal rate and paid more in actual tax dollars—obviously. In addition, from 2000 through 2005, income taxes paid by the wealthiest 20 percent increased from 81 percent of all income tax revenue to 86 percent despite no change in income distribution. This was a result of low-income "tax cuts" removing ten million filers from the income tax rolls.[1]

The success of the Reagan record is equally clear and indisputable. His tax cuts generated an unprecedented and sustained period of peacetime economic growth and prosperity—and it wasn't just the well-heeled who prospered. All income groups, from the lowest fifth to the highest fifth, did better. But leftists like Obama never tire of distorting the record. Why? Because class warfare still works in campaigns.

SPREADING THE MISERY

Obama made one of his most revealing anticapitalist statements during a primary debate with Hillary Clinton before the Pennsylvania primary. ABC's Charlie Gibson asked him about his support for an increase in the capital gains tax rates. Gibson pointed out—amazingly—that every time that capital gains rates had been decreased in the past, tax revenues from the tax increased and the government took in more money. Conversely, Gibson noted, when the rate was increased to 28 percent, revenues went down. "So why raise it at all, especially given the fact that one hundred million people in this country own stock and would be affected?"

Obama responded, "Well, Charlie, what I've said is that I would look at raising the capital gains tax for purposes of fairness."[2]

When I heard that, my jaw dropped open. I knew Obama was liberal, but this was a stunning admission. In his view, fairness is obviously defined by punishing higher income earners *even if it hurts everyone else as well.* There's no other way you can interpret the answer. The wealthy don't pay a lower rate than lower income earners and the poor wouldn't benefit if they paid a higher rate. But the fact that his proposed rate increase would result in less money to "spread around" to other people didn't bother him. His focus was on penalizing those he considered to be wealthy. Obama is so steeped in a class-warfare mentality that he didn't even realize how much his answer disclosed his prejudice against free-market capitalism. His economic philosophy is vintage liberalism: In his eyes, government, not the market, should pick the winners and losers. When individuals and businesses prosper in the free market it's inherently unfair—and this unfairness must be corrected, and, if possible, prevented by government.

How can Obama claim to be postpartisan and nondivisive when every fiber of his being exudes resentment toward the productive, successful, and well-off in society? I'm not exaggerating. In his first address to the nation, Obama said the Bush tax cuts were "an excuse to transfer wealth to the wealthy." He would correct this grievous injustice by increasing taxes on the "the wealthiest 2 percent of Americans." He condemned corporate executives for "greed" and "shirking a sense of responsibility."[3] He set up "special interests" and "lobbyists" as straw men opposing his Keynesian plan. "I know these steps won't sit well with the special interests and lobbyists who are invested in the old way of doing business, and I know they're gearing up for a fight as we speak. My message to them is this: 'So am I.' . . . The system we have now might work for the powerful and well-connected interests that have run Washington for far too long, but I don't. I work for the American people."[4]

How's that for unifying language? And how does that "old way of doing business" compare with Obama's way of doing business: ignoring the clear will of the public, bludgeoning and demonizing opponents of his agenda, distorting and concealing details of his programs, refusing to allow the public access to his and his party's legislation despite pledges of transparency, and attempting to rush bills through with scare tactics and constant fearmongering?

Obama's strategy in his first address was clever, if underhanded. He sought to put himself on the side of those who had no lobbyist in the power centers of government: the American people. He pledged to be their advocate against those "special interests" who would oppose "the sweeping change that this country demanded when it went to the polls in November." But it wasn't sweeping change the people wanted—not in the sense Obama implied. He had no mandate to turn America and its constitution upside down.

Nor would his economic plan bring about the types of change he promised: "change that will grow the economy, expand our middle-class, and keep the American dream alive for all those men and women who have believed in this journey from the day it began."

What could have been more Orwellian? Obama had no intention of keeping the American dream alive—unless by "American dream" you mean the dream of American leftist radicals to turn this nation into a full-blown socialist state. Conservatives knew at the time that his plans would not work to effect these results. Surely everyone can see it in retrospect: Keynesian pump-priming has never worked as a way to grow the American economy. It didn't work with the New Deal to end the Depression—indeed, it prolonged that economic disaster. And it greatly intensified the economic problems Obama is so anxious to tell us he inherited. You don't spend your way out of debt and you don't generate economic growth with artificially created, short-term government jobs.

"NOW IS NOT THE TIME FOR PROFITS"

What became clear, in a relatively short period of time, was that Obama was working against the American dream because he rejected it. It wasn't that he just had a different view of our way of life—it was that he simply didn't believe in the inherent fairness or goodness of the capitalistic system. He wasn't on the side of the American people, but was the champion of select special interests, such as unions, liberal academics, illegal immigrants, and anyone else he could entice to go along with his various plans—from the American Medical Association to the AARP to selected insurance companies and corporations. Once the American people discovered that he wasn't on their side, his messiah mystique quickly evaporated, along with his approval ratings.

In his inaugural address, Obama called for a new era of responsibility and condemned reports of what he considered excessive bonuses for executives of companies who had received bailout money. In a meeting in the Oval Office with his economic advisers, Obama ranted further on the subject. "That is the height of irresponsibility. It is shameful."

It was one thing for Obama to rail against bailout company executives receiving bonuses when their companies were suffering, but he went further—again revealing his instinctive distaste for our capitalistic system. "There will be a time for them to make profits, and there will be time for them to get bonuses—now is not that time. And that's a message I intend to send directly to them."[5] Obama's comments prompted CNBC *Mad Money* host Jim Cramer to draw comparisons between Obama and the Soviet Union's first leader, Vladimir Lenin. "Let me tell you something, we heard Lenin," Cramer said. "There was a little snippet last week that was, 'Now is not the time for profits.' Look—in Lenin's book, 'What Is to Be Done?' is simple text of what I always thought was [a key principle] for the communists. It was remarkable to hear very similar language from 'What Is to Be Done?' which is, We have no place for profits."[6]

It would have been some consolation if Obama's anticapitalism had ended at his class-divisive rhetoric, but that was not the case. His policies made his rhetoric look tame. According to the *Wall Street Journal*, Obama's stimulus bill would contain some $252 billion for income-transfer payments, including $83 billion to people who didn't earn enough to pay taxes.[7] Instead of counting those as spending increases, he deceitfully called them "tax cuts"—tax cuts for people not paying taxes—in order to misrepresent the bill's ratio of spending to tax cuts. Harvard economics professor Robert Barro said, "What they call tax reductions in this bill are really transfer payments, particularly redistribution of income from the rich to the poor." Unlike genuine tax cuts resulting from structural changes to the tax code, said Barro, these one-shot transfer payments would not stimulate economic growth.[8] As the Heritage Foundation's Brian Riedl noted, "Because tax credits do not reduce marginal tax rates for most taxpayers, they do not encourage the working, saving, and investing that are vital for productivity and growth." [9]

What made Obama's economic package brazenly cynical were his campaign promises (and postelection and poststimulus claims) of fiscal stewardship. During the campaign Obama said, "When I'm president, I will go line by line to make sure that we are not spending money unwisely." Yet very early in his presidency he signed a $410 billion omnibus spending bill that contained some nine thousand earmarks. His response to ABC's George Stephanopoulos was characteristically unapologetic: "We want to just move on. Let's get this bill done, get it into law and move forward." He tried to dismiss the rampant spending in the bill as just "last year's business," but that was a transparent cop-out: The bill was introduced and debated during Obama's watch, even if it did come under his predecessor's partial fiscal year. Whatever Clintonesque word games he tried to play, Obama's stimulus bill was as pork-laden as a smoked ham.

Obama further rationalized his signing of those bills by saying he would propose an earmark-free budget the next year. [10] Well, that promise didn't turn out too well, either: The earmarks for fiscal year 2010 would total some $12 billion. Even Democratic senator Russ Feingold pointed out that Obama had made earmark reform "a very big part of [his] campaign," yet still signed two spending measures including $4 billion in earmarks each. [11]

During the 2008 presidential campaign, in his second debate with Senator John McCain, Barack Obama promised the American people a "net spending cut." [12] And even after ramrodding his fiscal and stimulus packages through, and trying to pass cap-and-trade (which should really be called "cap-and-tax") and Obamacare, he still found a way to claim he was a deficit-conscious president. Amazing.

DEBT, DEBT, AND MORE DEBT

Obama's fraudulently labeled "stimulus bill" amounted to some $800 billion. But that was just the beginning. Though he promised to confront "tough choices" during the campaign, his first ten-year budget projection (for fiscal years 2010–2019) would amount to the largest debt-and-spending exercise in this nation's history. But instead of applying even a tinge of austerity, his budget projection the following year for the same period (2010–2019) was significantly worse. It would see spending increase an additional $1.7 trillion and budget deficits increase by an additional $2 trillion, as is shown on the Heritage Foundation graph below.[13] Indeed, Heritage's Brian Riedl observes that this year's ten-year proposal shows annual budget deficits as much as 49 percent larger than last year's—"raising the debt by an additional 6 percent of GDP over the same period."[14]

President Proposes $2 Trillion More in 2010–2019 Deficits Than Last Year

Proposed Budget Deficits, in Billions, by Fiscal Year

	Last Year's Budget Proposal	This Year's Budget Proposal
2010	−$1,258	−$1,556
2011	−$929	−$1,267
2012	−$557	−$829
2013	−$512	−$727
2014	−$536	−$706
2015	−$528	−$752
2016	−$645	−$778
2017	−$675	−$778
2018	−$688	−$785
2019	−$779	−$908
Total	−$7,107	−$9,086

Source: Table S-1 of President Obama's FY 2010 and FY 2011 budgets

Table 1 • WM 2787 ☎ heritage.org

Riedl also pointed out that Obama's projected ten-year budget would involve permanently expanding the federal government by almost 3 percent of GDP over the prerecession levels of 2007. It would increase taxes on all Americans by more than $2 trillion (factoring in his health care and cap and trade bills); increase taxes for 3.2 million small businesses and upper-income taxpayers an average of $300,000; borrow 42 cents for each dollar spent in 2010; run a 2010 budget deficit of some $1.6 trillion, which is $143 billion above the 2009 "recession-driven" deficit; see deficits in excess of $1 trillion as far as the eye can see—even as late as 2020; and double the publicly held national debt to above a staggering $18 trillion. It is breathtaking to realize that before the recession, federal spending amounted to $24,000 per household—but Obama wants to drive it to $36,000 per household by 2020, and that's *after* adjusting for inflation.[15]

Obama habitually criticized President Bush—always referred to as "my predecessor"—for leaving him with enormous deficits. But his own spending dwarfs Bush's. Bush's deficits averaged $300 billion annually; Obama's would be three or four times that—even after withdrawing from Iraq and beyond the time the economy was expected to recover, thus avoiding further extraordinary budget expenditures. Using Obama's own figures, President Bush's $3.3 trillion in deficits over eight years will be eclipsed by Obama's projected $7.6 trillion for his two terms—if, God forbid, there should be a second term. These deficits would cause net interest spending to reach $840 billion by 2020. And, as I've said many times on the air, the debt Obama would incur in that period would exceed that of all previous presidents combined. And some still wonder why we're crying out in protest!

Obama has never owned up to the significance of these

figures. Instead he tried again to mislead the public—this time through a numbers game. He has continually promised that he would cut his deficits in half by the end of his term. The only way that was mathematically possible, given his own first ten-year projected budget, would be to use the $1.4 trillion 2009 deficit as his baseline, ignoring all the extraordinary items that budget year contained. How difficult would it be to cut the deficit in half if the deficit amounted to $1.4 trillion in the year you were measuring other budget years against? How tough could it be to halve a budget after you've already quadrupled it? That's like the worst kind of retail fraud, where shady discount stores silently inflate their prices and then take out ads claiming they've slashed prices in half. But Obama's puffing didn't even have a one-year shelf life. His very next budget—for 2010—projected an increase in the deficit to $1.56 trillion.[16]

This bears repeating: It's grossly unfair for Obama to use the $1.4 trillion as the baseline deficit number when it contained extraordinary items from the bailouts and the stimulus, which would presumably be one-shot items. Apart from TARP, the deficits Obama inherited from President Bush were modest compared to the staggering levels he immediately increased them to—and they'll still be multiples higher than President Bush's at the end of Obama's term when, with luck, these extraordinary items will be long gone. As Brian Riedl writes, "One would expect the post-recession deficit to revert back to the $150 billion to $350 billion budget deficits that were typical before the recession. Instead, by 2019, the President forecasts a $917 billion budget deficit, a public debt of 77 percent of GDP, and annual net interest spending of $774 billion."[17] (And this assessment by Riedl was written before Obama's second ten-year budget, which involved much higher spending and larger deficits). And yet Obama expects "we the people" to give him kudos for his fiscal responsibility.

No matter which party you belong to, the point is that this country cannot continue to support this kind of debt. It's important for everyone to see through Obama's deceptive claims that his fiscal practices are no more reckless than those of his predecessor, or that they're necessary *because of* his predecessor. Both are grossly false. Obama's spending path is unsustainable, yet he plans on proceeding and even escalating it—he's talked of a second stimulus, he still plans to pass the enormously costly cap-and-tax and health-care bills, and he promised at the 2009 "climate change summit" in Copenhagen that the United States would give away $100 billion worth of aid to developing countries in the foreseeable future. There is no end in sight to Obama's profligate ways. It makes you wonder how anyone who cares about this country can even consider supporting his agenda.

Figures from the Office of Management and Budget showed that, in the 2009 budget year, the federal government would spend $30,958 per household. It would increase spending 22 percent to a peacetime record of 26 percent of the GDP. And this spending wouldn't be temporary: Obama's annual spending would remain five to eight thousand dollars higher per household than Bush's.[18]

MORTGAGE BAILOUT PLAN

The day after President Obama signed into law his $787 billion "stimulus" bill, he announced a separate $75 billion plan to bail out up to nine million families in jeopardy of losing their homes to foreclosure: the Home Affordable Modification Program. As usual, Obama billed the proposal as necessary to revive the economy—the same tack he has used with his stimulus package, his cap-and-trade proposal, and Obamacare. Every plan he proposes is integrally tied to every other program—and unless we accept the whole package, everything will fail, and we'll have an economic apocalypse on our hands. The plan involved little more than transfer payments to those who had either been irresponsible (though Obama denied that) or had seen their home equity evaporate when real estate prices tanked.

But there's an irony here: Many economists believe that the financial crisis that led to TARP and these other extraordinary economic measures was caused by the federal government's do-gooder policy of making homes available to almost everyone by forcing financial institutions to make irresponsible loans. Yet one of Obama's solutions—this mortgage bailout plan—would give us more of the same. It would do nothing to incentivize mortgage debtors to be more responsible and live within their means; it would do just the opposite. It would reward those borrowers, for what in many cases was their irresponsible behavior, with other people's money.

The plan outraged many people, even at this early stage in Obama's term. CNBC's Rick Santelli erupted into an eloquent rant denouncing the plan on live TV from the trading floor of the Chicago Board of Trade. Santelli said,

> The government is promoting bad behavior! . . . How about this, president and new administration: Why don't you put up a website to have people vote on the Internet as a referendum to see if we really want to subsidize the losers' mortgages, or would we like to at least buy cars and buy houses in foreclosure and give them to people that might have a chance to actually prosper down the road and reward people that could carry the

water instead of drink the water. . . . This is America! How many of you people want to pay for your neighbor's mortgage that has an extra bathroom and can't pay their bills? . . . President Obama, are you listening? . . . We're thinking of having a Chicago Tea Party in July. All of you capitalists that want to show up at Lake Michigan I'm going to start organizing it.[19]

In addition to being yet another unconstitutional confiscation of private property and transfer of wealth, Obama's grandiose mortgage bailout plan was an abject failure. The program, by all accounts, did not stop the rising tide of foreclosures. According to Politico, experts predicted that at least two million more homes would be lost before the end of 2009. Worse, the administration's plan to reach three to four million homes had fallen short by close to three or four million homes, in the grand tradition of big government; only about 160,000 of the homes it was designed to protect were covered. Even Democratic senator Chris Dodd, himself no innocent party in the nation's housing meltdown, said the Obama administration's progress in stopping foreclosures had been disgraceful.[20]

A nonpartisan research and policy organization, the Center for Responsible Lending, projected a minimum of 2.4 million additional foreclosures through 2009 with a resulting combined loss of $500 billion in property value to some 70 million surrounding homes. It estimated that by 2012 there would be 9 million foreclosures with $2 trillion worth of loss in surrounding property values.[21] All this after Obama's miraculous stimulus, enormous budget escalations, and special, targeted mortgage bailout plan.

Harvard law professor Elizabeth Warren, the "bailout watchdog" who heads a congressional oversight panel, said that the

Obama administration's signature foreclosure effort—the Home Affordable Modification Program (HAMP)—had fallen short. Through October 2009, only 10,187 homeowners had received permanent mortgage modifications, amounting to a mere 4.7 percent of those enrolled in three-month trial plans. This was a staggering failure, even by the administration's own standards. The Treasury had internally forecast that as many as 75 percent of the trial participants would transition to permanent status.[22] The panel concluded that "one factor contributing to the paucity of permanent modifications is issues in gathering borrower documentation. HAMP trial modifications can be initiated before homeowners provide any documentation of their income and assets and that documentation, which in many cases borrowers did not have to show in order to get their original loans, is required to be produced before a loan modification can exit the trial period." In other words, liberalism's faith in big government to work miracles was once again roundly discredited.[23]

The panel confessed its concern that even the homeowners who receive permanent modification status might re-default and ultimately lose their homes to foreclosure. And Warren reported that only ten of the seventy-nine mortgage services enrolled in the program have been paid for successfully modifying loans on a permanent basis.

The bottom line is this: The mortgage bailout program was touted as likely to help three to four million homeowners avoid foreclosure through mortgage modification that would lower their monthly payments. But with the high unemployment rate, mounting foreclosures, and homeowners owing more than their properties are worth, Warren proclaimed that the program just "isn't working." The panel's estimate for future foreclosures was as bleak as that of the Center for Responsible Lending: The panel projected that foreclosures would range from 8.1 million in the next four years to as many as 13 million in the next five-plus years.

THE STIMULUS BUST

When Obama was unveiling his economic plans, he assured us that, because of his intervention, unemployment would not rise above 8 percent, and that it should "save or create at least 3 million jobs by the end of 2010"—as if "saving" jobs were a measurable statistic. (It's revealing that the mainstream media, as in-the-tank for Obama as they are, still allow him to get away with such a bogus ruse.) On January 10, 2009, Christina Romer, Obama's designated chair of the Council of Economic Advisers, issued a report called "The Job Impact of the American Recovery and Reinvestment Plan," setting the job figures at more optimistic levels. The president's plan, she wrote, "is expected to create between three and four million jobs by the end of 2010," and "more than 90 percent of the jobs created are likely to be in the private sector."

But the Obama brain trust failed at every turn. The Bureau of Labor Statistics reported on November 6, 2009, that unemployment had skyrocketed to 10.2 percent in October—the highest rate since 1983. The tone-deaf and veracity-challenged administration maintained, in spite of these figures, that it had "created or saved" 640,000 jobs. Vice President Joe Biden even bragged that the stimulus package was "doing more, faster, more efficiently, and more effectively than most expected." But even the administration's own website, Recovery.org, contradicted these absurd boasts, reporting that only 30,383 jobs had been created or saved by the stimulus fiasco.[24]

The truth was that 2.8 million jobs had been *lost* since the stimulus bill was enacted.[25] Moreover, most of the jobs that *were* created were not in the private sector, as predicted, but in the public sector—and, worse, they were mostly temporary.[26] Some experts, such as Peter Morici, an economist and business professor at the University of Maryland, said that from the beginning the bill was mostly designed to create public sector jobs, contradicting the administration's claim.[27]

Even more embarrassing to the administration—especially in view of Biden's assurances that he would personally police the proper expenditure of stimulus monies—was that Recovery.org showed millions of federal stimulus dollars being sent to congressional districts that did not exist. Rhode Island's 86th district received $10.2 million in stimulus funds to save 57.9 jobs, and Connecticut's 42nd was able to save 25 jobs. Unfortunately for the Obama administration and stimulus cop Joe Biden, Rhode Island has only two congressional districts; Connecticut has five.[28]

New Mexico Watchdog, a project of the Rio Grande Foundation, a research institute, has reported on other irregularities with the stimulus funding. It too caught the administration claiming to have created jobs for congressional districts that didn't exist—this time in New Mexico—but it didn't stop there. As Watchdog's Jim Scarantino reported, "First it was phantom Congressional districts. Now it's phantom zip codes." Scarantino reports the administration claims to have created jobs and sent money to zip codes that do not exist. Some $6.4 billion was reported as being allocated to 440 nonexistent districts, he said. Scarantino added this indictment: "As in the case of the phantom Congressional districts, the dollar magnitude of the errors we found in little New Mexico was eclipsed by the repetition of these glaring reporting errors across the nation. If we can find nonexistent zip codes, we have no doubt that our counterparts in other states, which have received much more money, will again be able to repeat and expand upon our results." [29]

Updates on Watchdog's website showed that West Virginia's Watchdog reported $28 million in stimulus funds going to nonexistent zip codes. Nebraska's also found millions allocated to these phantom zip codes, and Washington state reported the same problem.

Beyond the fraud there is the enormous, outrageous waste. As just one set of examples, the *Oakland Tribune* reported the following allocations of stimulus money for its area: $50,000 for a nonprofit best known for its fiery performance art; $54 million to protect train tracks for hauling tourists through vineyards as they sip wine in Napa County; $272,578 to provide housing assistance to two Native American tribes that "reap millions a year from lucrative gambling casinos in Sonoma County"; and $499,384 for field studies to determine what kind of alcohol young people imbibe in bars and other hot spots. [30]

On top of that, we know that much of the stimulus money, and other federal monies under the control of this administration, have been used not to revive the economy, or to help the poor, but for the old-fashioned purpose of reelecting Obama's Democrats. Columnist Mona Charen has noted that the federal government has announced plans to spend $340 million on an advertising campaign to promote the census—including $2.5 million for Super Bowl ads. [31] As Charen quipped, "Though the nation has been collecting this data for 220 years, it seems we now need commercial jingles to complete the forms. Or," she asks, "could there be another agenda? The government . . . will target $80 million of those dollars to racial and ethnic minorities and non-English speakers—groups that vote disproportionately Democratic. Nor will Democrats permit efforts to limit the count to those here legally. An effort by Sen. David Vitter (R-LA) to exclude illegal aliens from the count went nowhere." Mona noted that Democratic congressional districts are receiving 1.6 times more stimulus money on average than Republican ones. She confirmed that the overwhelming majority of the stimulus funds have been allocated to the public sector, not the private sector.

Is the stimulus starting to sound like a slush fund? Chilling stuff.

Even if all the stimulus money had been channeled into "stimulus" purposes, of course it still wouldn't have worked— because Keynesian economics doesn't work. As the Heritage Foundation's Brian Riedl has pointed out, Congress cannot inject money into the economy until it has first borrowed that money out of the economy. In his paper "Why Government Spending Does Not Stimulate Economic Growth," he shatters the fallacies that Keynesians use to defend government spending as stimulus. Among other things, Riedl shows that simple math disproves the theory. He notes that if each dollar of additional deficit spending increases GDP by $1.50, as contended by economist Mark Zandi in his successful pitch to congressmen in support of the stimulus plan, then "last year's $1 trillion increase in the budget deficit would have created an enormous $1.5 trillion in new wealth (in a $14 trillion economy, this would have not only ended the recession, it would have caused massive overheating). Instead the economy shrank by $300 billion." [32]

In retrospect, then, we have the empirical data to prove that Obama's stimulus plan was both a fraud and a miserable, destructive failure. Of course, many of us knew well when he launched it that it wasn't about stimulating the economy, but about redistribution of wealth, political payoffs, and developing a war chest for future Democratic election efforts. Obama always blamed the economic crisis he inherited for his record spending plans, but the truth is that the financial meltdown was just an excuse, a convenient backdrop for his socialistic schemes. When it fell into his lap, the crisis gave him an occasion to press forward with a plan he had envisioned for years. Anyone who doubts this need only consult the haunting words of his adviser, Rahm Emanuel: "You don't ever want a crisis to go to waste; it's an opportunity to do important things that you would otherwise avoid."

Even if government could create significant numbers of jobs through borrowing and printing money—which history has shown it can't—Obama's plan never even contemplated spending most of the money in time to do much stimulating. The plan, from the outset, was backloaded. By the end of fiscal 2009 (September 30), 78 percent of the federal spending that the bill authorized—$173 billion of the $787 billion—had not yet occurred, according to a November report of the Government Accountability Office (GAO). In its December 2009 report to Congress, the GAO reported that states had only spent one-quarter of the funds set aside for them in the stimulus.

This is especially troubling when you consider that Obama sold his stimulus package through fearmongering, grimly warning that it was urgent that Congress pass the "recovery" bill immediately. He insisted that the fate of the economy completely depended on passing the bill so that federal monies could be injected into the economy to create jobs. In a speech from the White House on February 6, 2009, he lamented a new report from the Labor Department indicating that 3.6 million jobs had been lost since the recession began. He said, "I am sure that at the other end of Pennsylvania Avenue, members of the Senate are reading these same numbers this morning. I hope they share my sense of urgency and draw the same, unmistakable conclusion: the situation could not be more serious. These numbers demand action. It is inexcusable and irresponsible to get bogged down in distraction and delay while millions of Americans are being put out of work. It is time for Congress to act. It is time to pass an Economic Recovery and Reinvestment Plan to get our economy moving again."

He had made the argument even more pointedly on January 16, before his inauguration: "The way I see it, the first job of my administration is to put people back to work and get our economy moving again," said Obama. "That's why I've moved quickly to work with my economic team and leaders of both parties on an American Recovery and Reinvestment Plan that will immediately jump-start job creation and long-term growth."[33] There's no question that Obama made a direct causal connection between his bill, the money it would circulate, and job creation. This kind of empty rhetoric is his stock in trade: Nearly a year later, *after his stimulus plan had failed,* he used the very same terms in a speech, telling the American people that he would be sending Congress ideas for "jump-starting" the economy.[34] It's as though he were a talking windup toy with no new audio tapes.

Obama was undaunted by the manifest failure of his stimulus package at every level. Instead of apologizing to the American people for his colossal waste of money, Obama, as I mentioned earlier, called for a White House jobs summit—as if he hadn't been promising to fix the unemployment problem for more than a year. But this job summit obviously wasn't about convening his fellow economic geniuses in academia and selective businesses to brainstorm about job creation. It was a PR gambit, a photo op designed to stop the hemorrhaging in his approval ratings, which were destined to get worse because of these abysmal jobs reports. The participants were like-minded big-government leftists, and the outcome was preordained. The result was just one more in Obama's Long Parade of Summits—on top of his "fiscal responsibility summit," his "health care summit," his "swine flu summit," his "distracted driving summit," and his "beer summit." "It's not that I've got summit-itis here," he protested. Could have fooled us, Mr. President.

A few short weeks later, in a speech to the Brookings Institution, Obama again displayed his signature audacity—by calling for a second stimulus![35] Surely it never dawned on this hopelessly liberal ideologue that he should instead consider a course correction, a new effort to unleash the private sector and let the market work its magic. His single-minded determination, and refusal to acknowledge reality, were mind-boggling. The only remaining question was Barack Obama's real motivation: Was he really trying to accomplish the largest federal power grab in memory—or was he deliberately trying to dismantle and destroy the American economy?

CAP-AND-TRADE

One common theme that runs through the liberal legislation proposed in the Obama era is that it contemplates vast increases in the scope and role of government, and in how much control government has on our lives—all of this *without* accomplishing what Obama promises it will. The ostensibly environmen-tally motivated cap-and-trade bill is said to be about reducing carbon emissions to reduce their supposed impact on global warming—which, the argument goes, will otherwise kill us all us in the not-too-distant future. Even if you accept the environmentalists' premises, the proposals don't appreciably reduce global emissions, and they would have negligible impact on global temperature, even in the long run. But the cap-and-trade bill would have an enormously detrimental impact on major pillars of our society: our fiscal solvency, our national sovereignty, and our liberty. The same is true of Obamacare: The driving impetus for Obama's health-care legislation is that too many are uninsured and we pay too much for too little quality. But Obamacare, even if it went swimmingly, would leave *millions* uninsured; it would increase the overall costs of health care; it would result in rationing; and it would reduce the quality of care. Even worse, it would exponentially expand the scope of government and dramatically reduce our freedom. None of these inevitable results bothers liberals, of course, because they judge themselves—and others—not on results, but on their supposedly good intentions. But their results could wreck the American way of life.

Cap-and-trade is a prime example. Given the kinds of Draconian remedies that the left has suggested to combat global warming, you'd think Congress would conduct its own independent investigation into the truth behind the theories about man-made global warming and what, if any, kind of harm it represents. Instead, arrogant liberals, flanked by their media mouthpieces, refuse to explore the issue, telling us that the scientific question has been "settled" by "consensus" and that they'll no longer condescend even to humor us in a discussion of the matter. Case closed.

Their unilateral declaration of a consensus must feel gratifying to them, but it doesn't make it so. More than 31,000 scientists, more than 9,000 of whom hold Ph.D.s, have signed a petition urging the United States to reject the global warming agreement known as the Kyoto Protocols—and similar proposals (such as Kyoto II, which issued from Copenhagen in 2009)—because "the proposed limits on greenhouse gases would harm the environment, hinder the advance of science and technology, and damage the health and welfare of mankind." One hundred scientists endorsed a newspaper ad by the Cato Institute challenging the president's "facts" on global warming. In their penchant for psychological projection, the global warming liberals accuse skeptics (they call them "deniers" and worse) of ignoring the hard science because they're in the pocket of the special interests. In fact, as the eruption of Climategate last year dramatically confirmed for us, it is the consensus promoters themselves who have a vested interest in perpetuating all the public hysteria over their mythical claims.

The role of political correctness, intimidation, and good old-fashioned peer pressure on the academic left can't be overstated. As MIT's Richard Lindzen has acknowledged, many scientists refuse to publicize their dissent simply to make "their lives easier." Even before Climategate, CBS's Political Hotsheet revealed that

> the Environmental Protection Agency may have suppressed an internal report that was skeptical of claims about global warming, including whether carbon dioxide must be strictly regulated by the federal government, according to a series of newly disclosed e-mail messages. . . . Less than two weeks before the agency formally submitted its pro-regulation recommendation to the White House, an EPA center director quashed a 98-page report that warned against making hasty "decisions based on a scientific hypothesis that does not appear to explain most of the available data." [36]

For many Americans, though, it was the Climategate story itself that gave smoking-gun support to our long-held suspicions about the legitimacy of the global warming scientific establishment.

Climategate involved the Internet publication in November 2009 of 1,073 e-mails and nearly 3,600 other documents from the University of East Anglia's Climatic Research Unit (CRU), a center for climate data storage and analysis in the United Kingdom. Its director, Dr. Phil Jones, is one of the main authors of Intergovernmental Panel on Climate Change AR4 report that has served as the basis for the global push to limit carbon emissions.[37]

The e-mails and other documents that were published in Climategate reveal a conspiracy among many of the movers and shakers in the climate science community to a) avoid peer review of papers favorable to their preferred theory of manmade global warming and suppress publication of papers with an opposing view; and b) cherry-pick and distort data and the analysis of data to align it with their preferred theory.[38] The scandal led to the resignations and investigations of top scientists in England and the United States and to the British government's decision to recalculate its historic weather findings.[39] It's ironic that those who claim that the evidence of manmade global warming is indisputable nevertheless felt the need to manipulate the very data they say proves their theory.

Beyond these Climategate conspirators' decision to resort to sordid tactics, and their refusal to weigh the science objectively, the climate-change zealots also refuse to entertain a serious discussion about how much, if any, their proposed bills would reduce global warming, or whether reductions would have any measurable impact on human health.

Nor are they always honest about the prohibitive costs their proposals would entail—although even the slickest of them have been known to slip, as when Obama admitted to a *San Francisco Chronicle* reporter that his cap-and-trade proposal would bankrupt the coal industry.[40] If they were consistently forthright about the costs of their proposals, their ideas would be dead *before* arrival.

Sadly, many on our side of the ideological spectrum have allowed themselves to be bullied into conceding the fundamental premise that man-made (anthropogenic) global warming is going to destroy the planet and its human inhabitants unless we take dramatic steps to reverse the course of modern civilization and buy a one-way ticket back into the Stone Age. For them to give up the battle this way is not only unwarranted, it's criminal.

There is an abundance of scientific evidence contradicting the environmentalists' hysterical claims. In a speech to the Heartland Institute's Third International Conference on Climate Change on June 2, 2009, the Heritage Foundation's Ben Lieberman pointed out "that both the seriousness and imminence of anthropogenic global warming has been overstated." Moreover, he said, the Waxman-Markey cap-and-trade proposal "would have a trivial impact on future concentrations of greenhouse gases. It would reduce the earth's temperature by 0.1 to 0.2 degree C by 2100, an amount too small to even notice." The United States would be the only country whose standards would be constrained by the bill, and "the trends in the rest of the world show clearly that emissions are rising. China alone now out-emits the U.S. and it hasn't just inched ahead, it has raced ahead with emissions rising six times faster than ours. A similar story is true of other rapidly developing nations," said Lieberman.[41] The European nations that have already imposed similar restrictions on carbon emissions have seen their emissions rise—hardly a testament to the efficacy of such proposals, but surely no deterrent to well-meaning liberals nevertheless.

Even the best-case analyses predict negligible results for cap-and-trade. Yet the projected costs of the idea are staggering beyond measure. Experts from the Heritage Foundation estimate that the direct costs would be an average of $829 per year for a household of four—that's a total cost of $20,000 between 2012 and 2035. But when you factor in the cost of allocations and offsets, the average cost to the family would be *$2,979 per year* during that same period. And who would be hurt worst by the legislation? The poor, because they would bear a disproportionately higher share of the energy costs the bill would generate. The bill would devastate the manufacturing sector, causing an average of 1.15 million in net job losses between 2012 and 2030. We would sustain losses to the GDP averaging $393 billion annually from 2012 to 2035, with a cumulative GDP loss of $9.4 trillion by 2035. By the year 2035, the average family's share of the national debt would increase by $115,000.[42]

None of this evidence seeps through the closed psyche of the impervious left. To the contrary, Paul Krugman of the *New York Times* condemns anyone who questions cap-and-trade: "As I watched the [global warming] deniers make their arguments, I couldn't help thinking that I was watching a form of treason—treason against the planet."

Meanwhile, Qing-Bin Lu, a credible Canadian physicist and astronomer at the University of Waterloo, has released a peer-reviewed study that attributes the global warming trend of the twentieth century to the interaction of cosmic rays and chlorofluorocarbons—and, with the diminution of CFCs in recent years, we're already seeing a halt to the warming and global cooling trends that could extend for the next half century. According to Qing, the cooling trend began in 2002, and "the observed data show that CFCs conspiring with cosmic rays most likely caused both the Antarctic ozone hole and global warming. These findings are totally unexpected and striking, as I was focused on studying the mechanism for the formation of the ozone hole, rather than global warming."[43]

Will the American left ever show the same open-mindedness Qing-Bin demonstrated in seeing the truth behind the data—even when the scientific establishment would have preferred he look the other way?

OBAMACARE

As a leftist to his core, Barack Obama has been salivating over socialized medicine for years. It's the perfect policy vehicle for socialists who want to ensure that government's tentacles will spread into all aspects of our society. They have been trying for decades to impose it on this liberty-loving nation. It is the socialists' dream, a solution that has all the attributes of Trojan-horse liberalism: It appears perfectly compassionate on the drawing board, while operating as a freedom vacuum once put into practice.

Ronald Reagan warned against socialized medicine as early as 1961, when he was working with the then-rational American Medical Association to oppose the Democratic Party's efforts to establish it. As Reagan said then, "One of the traditional methods of imposing statism or socialism on a people has been by way of medicine. It's very easy to disguise a medical program as a humanitarian project. . . . Now, the American people, if you put it to them about socialized medicine and gave them a chance to choose, would unhesitatingly vote against it."[44]

What do you know? Once again Reagan's words have proven timeless. When Obama began his propaganda campaign stumping for this crown jewel of his domestic agenda, his plans for "universal coverage" were very popular with the American people—as was Obama himself. But once the truth about socialized medicine began coming out, the public spoke in a loud voice against the measure. The more Obama himself spoke publicly on the subject, the less support his program—and he himself—enjoyed.

In the first few months of his presidency, 63 percent of voters agreed with Obama's general push for universal health-care coverage.[45] But as his first year was coming to a close, Rasmussen Reports said that 56 percent opposed Obamacare, and 46 percent strongly opposed it, while only 19 percent strongly favored it. Sixty-three percent of senior citizens opposed the plan, and 52 percent strongly opposed it.[46]

The trend in the president's personal approval ratings was equally bleak. In early January 2009, 65 percent approved and only 30 percent disapproved of his performance, but by December 24, 2009, only 44 percent approved while 56 percent disapproved. When he began, 44 percent *strongly* approved and 16 percent *strongly* disapproved. Yet by December 24, 43 percent strongly disapproved and only 27 percent strongly approved.[47]

Despite Obama's nonstop lobbying against the existing health-care system, and his promises that his plan would not increase taxes and would increase the quality of care, 74 percent of voters continued to believe their health care was good or excellent and 50 percent believed Obamacare would lead to a decline in their care. A full 78 percent of people outright disbelieved Obama's claims that his plan wouldn't result in higher taxes for the middle class.[48] But he nevertheless pressed forward, disregarding the expressed wishes of the people. On Christmas Eve, the Democrat-controlled Senate passed health-care legislation by a 60-39 strict party line vote. Just before the vote, Senate Majority Leader Harry Reid said the bill was what the American people "have deserved for six and a half decades," and he predicted that lawmakers would hear "an earful of joy and happiness." Minority Leader Mitch McConnell called the bill a "monstrosity." Reid's comments typified the arrogance that had come to characterize Obama and his party, along with their flagrant disregard for the wishes of the people: "Our charge is to move forward," he said. "Though some may slow the progress, they cannot stop it."[49]

After the Christmas recess, the Democrats became even more secretive and dismissive of the people's wishes and interests. In order to streamline final passage of a bill approved by both chambers, Senate and House Democrats went behind closed doors and set in motion a plan to bypass traditional legislative procedures to exclude Republicans from the process. The normal process is for a House-Senate conference committee to reconcile differences in the two versions of the legislation. These compromise talks would include just three small groups: top Democrats in the House, top Democrats in the Senate, and White House representatives.[50]

So much for bipartisanship. So much for transparency. So much for democratic government. Smelling a rat, even the scrupulously nonpartisan C-SPAN weighed in, reminding President Obama of his pledge to conduct health-care negotiations publicly on the network. C-SPAN CEO Brian Lamb wrote a letter to Obama and congressional leaders, saying, "many of your rank-and-file members, and the nation's editorial pages have all talked about the value of transparent discussions on reforming the nation's health care system. Now that the process moves to the critical stage of reconciliation between the Chambers, we respectfully request that you allow the public full access, through television, to legislation that will affect the lives of every single American."[51] This was hardly an unreasonable request, considering that Obama was on videotape no fewer than eight times during the campaign promising to conduct health-care negotiations in public and in front of the cameras.

AN AGENDA BASED ON DECEIT

This mockery of transparency and good and honest government should have come as no surprise. Obama's health-care agenda had always been based on lies—the keystone of which was his contention that his health-care reform package was crucial to our overall economic recovery. As he said, "Reforming our health care is a critical step in rebuilding our economy so that entrepreneurs can pursue the American dream again and our small businesses can grow and expand and create new jobs again." His illustrious vice president, Joe Biden, took one step further—into scare tactics. He told one AARP audience that if we didn't pass Obamacare, the nation's finances would collapse. "And, folks, look, AARP knows and the people with me here today know, the president knows, and I know, that the status quo is simply not acceptable. It's totally unacceptable. And it's completely unsustainable. Even if we wanted to keep it the way we have it now. It can't do it financially," he said. "We're going to go bankrupt as a nation. . . . Now, people, when I say that look at me and say,

'What are you talking about, Joe? You're telling me we have to go spend money to keep from going bankrupt?' " Biden said. "The answer is yes, that's what I'm telling you." [52]

Obama contended that his plan was about increasing patient choice, not government control. He said that the public option was just a part of that effort, that it would increase the public's choices. He said he wasn't adamant about achieving a single-payer system, and that the public option would not be a Trojan horse for a single-payer system. He denigrated the quality of American health care. He grossly misrepresented the number of people who were uninsured. He promised, "I will not sign a plan that adds one dime to our deficits either now or in the future—period," and that he would not increase taxes on the middle class. He said that his plan would not include public funding for abortions and that it would preserve the conscience protections currently afforded health-care providers. He said that his plan would not involve rationing ("Don't pay attention to those scary stories about how your benefits will be cut. . . . That will never happen on my watch") or "death panels," and that it would improve the quality of health care and extend affordable care to all Americans. He said that his plan would not cover illegal immigrants, that no one would be forced to buy health care, and that no one would be forced out of plans they already liked ("Let me repeat this: nothing in our plan requires you to change what you have"). He said that government could control health-care costs better than the private sector. And he said that he'd bring all parties together to negotiate the final version on cable TV. [53]

All of these were lies. The Obama Democrats were determined to achieve socialized medicine by any means necessary, and they weren't about to let the truth get in their way of delivering an agenda for the American people they knew was in the people's best interests even if they were too ignorant to realize it themselves.

The driving premise of the Democrats' push to nationalize health care has been centered on the myths they've propagated about the numbers of uninsured. The Clintons started popularizing this canard, but Obama pressed it to new heights. Their premise was that 47 million Americans were uninsured and unable to obtain insurance. Yet according to many health-care experts, such as Sally Pipes, this number is grossly inflated. Many included in that number—almost half—remain uninsured for an average of four months. In fact, roughly 38 percent of the uninsured can afford coverage (some 18 million of them make more than $50,000 a year, and 10 million of those make more than $75,000), but choose, for their own reasons (trusting in their youth and good health and favoring other priorities), not to get it. Millions more of the uninsured are noncitizens. Then there's a core truth that's unbearably painful for liberals: "as many of the 14 million of the 45.7 million uninsured—poor and low-income Americans—are fully eligible for generous government assistance programs like Medicare, Medicaid, and SCHIP," but "they're just not enrolling in the programs." When Obama cries that almost 8 million children are without health insurance, he fails to reveal that 5 million of them go without only because they haven't been enrolled in available programs.

When you remove all those red herrings, Pipes estimates, the number of people who are "chronically uninsured" is probably close to 8 million—not 45.7 million or 47 million.[54] Of course that just wouldn't sell as well. But it's astonishing to realize that no matter which of the horrible Obama-style plans the Democrats pushed for in their months-long health-care "reform" campaign, *all of them* would have resulted in millions upon millions of Americans remaining uninsured—*after Obama's changes were fully implemented.*

If Obama really wanted to improve health care in this country, why would he back such fundamentally flawed programs? Because his goal has never been to increase choice in health care. He is on record as saying that he favors a single-payer plan. Even Democratic congressman Barney Frank has said that the public option was about establishing a single-payer plan. As we saw in some of the early plans Obama supported, the public option was legislatively designed to crowd out the private sector by stacking the deck in favor of the public plan. He said that people wouldn't be forced out of plans they liked, but most people had employer-based plans, and employers would be incentivized to adopt the public plan. Once people lost their current plan, they would be prevented from reacquiring coverage in a private plan thereafter, so it was just a matter of time before the private plans would be phased out entirely—at the behest of the federal government. A provision in an early House bill would have invested the government with power to audit employers who didn't take Obama's hint to adopt the public option and retained their self-insurance.

As for Obama's claim that federal funds wouldn't be used for abortion, the truth is that every attempt by congressmen to add language prohibiting the practice was defeated by Obama's Democrats. The bill the Senate passed on Christmas Eve included major taxpayer funding of abortion and, some said, opened the door for the administration to force insurance companies to pay for abortions.[55]

Obama says almost gleefully that Americans pay $6,000 more per year on health care than people of other advanced nations for no better care. "We are the only advanced democracy on earth . . .

that allows such hardships for millions of its people. . . . We spend one and a half times more per person on health care than any other country, but we aren't any healthier for it."

Contrary to Obama's statements, America has the best health-care system in the world. Senator Tom Coburn has aptly stated that if America had established a government-run system like Canada's or Britain's ten years ago, there would be one million fewer Americans alive today. Because of our available technology and acute intervention, "our survival rates on cancer, malignancies and coronary artery disease" are better than Canada's or Britain's.[56] Indeed—much as Obama seems anxious to find fault with America, and seems to regard every other nation with awe—he conveniently ignores that America leads the world in treating heart disease and cancer and that America's medical research industry produces more than half of the $175 billion of health-care technology products purchased globally. In 2004, Sally Pipes notes, the U.S. government spent $18.4 billion on medical research; the European Union, with a larger population, spent only $3.7 billion.[57] As some have observed, "Europeans are living off the US taxpayer in health care, as in so many things."[58]

Moreover, if America were to implement socialized care, the quality of our health care would necessarily decrease. How do we know this? Because it's been the case with every nation that has tried it. Economists uniformly tell us that price controls (which are part of Obamacare) always reduce quality, because they reduce the incentive to provide quality. Anyone who doubts this should read the horror stories from British hospitals.[59]

And the financial aspects of this nightmare are at least as horrifying. Obama insisted that his plan wouldn't add to the federal deficit, but no one believed him—and for good reason. Most of the plans scored by the Congressional Budget Office (CBO) were found to have increased the deficit. Worse yet, those that *didn't* were often based on incomplete information provided to the CBO in order to get a favorable result. CBO has to operate with the numbers it is given: garbage in, garbage out.

But even in those few plans that were scored neutrally, what the naked CBO scoring couldn't tell you is that cost estimates for government programs *are always* understated. In 1965 the government projected that costs for Medicare Part A would be $9 billion; they ended up being $67 billion. The Medicaid special hospitals subsidy of $11 billion was one hundred times greater than the government's projections that it would cost $100 million. The idea that price controls reduce costs is another myth. As Dr. Thomas Sowell explains, price controls don't eliminate costs; they just help make some of them less visible in the short run. These artificially lower prices will encourage more demand while decreasing supply—which will lead to shortages and rationing. And, after all, who could be so gullible as to believe that adding millions of people to the health-care rolls, while insulating them from price considerations, would cause costs and prices to fall? Just because some of those costs are shifted to the private sector by government mandate doesn't mean they aren't still costs, burdens carried by the people.

Proponents of socialized medicine always present their plans as being driven by compassion, but they are anything but. Under such plans, government always increases its mandates. Obamacare would force people to purchase insurance who don't want to buy it, and would increase certain treatments that have to be covered even though no one would reasonably consider them to be medical necessities. This increased demand, compelled by law, would jack up prices across the board. Sally Pipes has documented that already existing government laws do just that. In 1979, she said, there were only 252 mandates in force in health care; by 2007 there were some 1900. Things like massage therapy, breast reduction, and hair prosthesis were mandated, largely as a result of special interest lobbying—the type of thing liberals tell you they shun.

But we don't have to rely only on economics maxims to demonstrate that Obamacare would involve rationing. The drafters of the legislation knew that well—so well that they incorporated a mechanism to deal with it. One of the early iterations of Obamacare (H.R. 3200) would have established a government committee to recommend a benefits package replete with dollar limitations on coverage for the recommended treatments. Many expressed serious concerns about provisions in the bill encouraging end-stage counseling—anticipating the built-in conflict of interest the government would surely face if it were responsible for both controlling costs and counseling people about expensive care that could extend their lives. Besides, the bill's drafters seemed just as concerned with political correctness as health care: They included a provision that the committee should include experts in "racial and ethnic disparities," an idea right out of the Obama "postracial" playbook.

Democrats were finally able to cobble together a majority in the Senate for their Obamacare bill passed in the early morning of December 24. But they didn't do it through Obama's or Harry Reid's negotiation skills. They resorted to good old-fashioned quid pro quo, acquiring recalcitrant senators' votes at the last possible minute in a despicable display of political corruption. A month earlier, Louisiana senator Mary Landrieu's support had been obtained after the government promised $300 million in special aid to her state—a move that came to be known as the

"Louisiana Purchase." Likewise, Democrats secured Senator Ben Nelson's vote with a special Medicaid break for Nebraska that would continue in perpetuity. Nelson and Michigan senator Carl Levin both secured special tax exemptions for insurers in their states. Further, aid covering Medicaid expansion costs were secured for Vermont and Massachusetts, and Senator Chris Dodd prevailed on his colleagues to insert in the bill a $100 million plum for construction of a university hospital in Connecticut. And Pennsylvania, New York, and Florida were all able to procure protections for their Medicare Advantage beneficiaries—at a time when that program was facing nationwide cuts.[60]

Conservatives, outraged at this blatant corruption, threatened to challenge the bill on constitutional grounds. Richard Epstein, a constitutional scholar at the University of Chicago, argued that the newly passed Senate bill was unconstitutional. He focused on the protections under the Bill of Rights that prevent government "takings" without just compensation and deprivation of property without due process of law, among other things. Other scholars argued that Congress was overstepping its authority under the Commerce Clause by forcing Americans to purchase health insurance. When confronted with complaints about the unconstitutionality of their legislation, liberal congressmen and congresswomen routinely dismissed the concern—as if to say they recognize no limitations on their power "to do good" for the American people.

The more we learn about the Senate's Christmas Eve boondoggle, the more disturbing it becomes. My friend Betsey McCaughey, former lieutenant governor of New York and founder of the Committee to Reduce Infection Deaths, has studied the bill carefully. In a scathing critique published at Investors.com, she compiled a list of the top things you don't want from health-care reform but will receive anyway: higher premiums, including 10 to 13 percent more per year for those paying for their own insurance; a mandatory requirement to purchase insurance for those who might otherwise opt out—and penalties to enforce it; a one-size-fits-all plan no matter how much you're taxed for it; a punitive tax on employers who provide better packages (in keeping with Obama's philosophy of equalizing outcomes and spreading the misery); and a requirement that doctors, in order to participate in the private insurance system, must implement government regulations concerning the quality of health care. (So much for Obama not interfering with the doctor-patient relationship!)

As McCaughey point out, this would be the first time in history that the federal government would have power over: a) how doctors treat privately insured patients; b\) reductions in payments to hospitals and other facilities that care for seniors; c) hospital budget cuts (as the president's chief health adviser, Dr. Ezekiel Emanuel, says, the United States has an "abundance of amenities" compared to Europe, which drives up costs here; d) future Medicare cuts; e) a new social agenda, with money allocated for adult preparation activities and the like as well as giveaways to immigrants; and f) a sharing of electronic records between doctors, which would entail a gross encroachment on our privacy.[61]

SOLUTIONS

Democrats say Republicans are just the Party of No, that critics of the plan have offered no constructive solutions for health-care problems. That's simply not true: Republicans *do* have market-based solutions, but none of them will make it past the cutting room floor of Congress, because of the overwhelming Democratic majorities. As with their track record in so many policy areas, Democrats have already created enormous problems on health care by expanding government control. Medicare, Medicaid, veterans' care, tax laws incentivizing employers to provide health care for employees, excessive mandates, and other regulations have all greatly damaged the health-care industry. Democrats want to remedy that with more of the same.

What we need is *less* government and a vigorous reintroduction of market forces into the medical industry. We need to reverse tax laws that make health-care costs invisible to the employee, and to reconnect price with demand. We need to repeal the laws that put these onerous mandates in place, and those that prevent purchasing insurance across state lines. We need to expand health savings accounts and adopt tort reform.

There is little doubt that President Obama's free-falling approval ratings are tied to the American people's growing concern over his socialistic policies. American taxpayers are alarmed at his refusal to rein in federal spending even as he admits that his current budgets are unsustainable; at his federal power grabs, including his takeover of large segments of the automobile industry; at his high-handed treatment of creditors, such as Chrysler, with whom he pretended to be negotiating in good faith and then smeared as a "small group of speculators [who] endanger Chrysler's future by refusing to sacrifice like everyone else"; and at his demonization of "big oil," insurance companies, pharmaceutical companies, corporate executives, the legitimate taking of profits, Tea Party protesters, global warming skeptics, the CIA, the military, capitalists, the wealthy, conservative radio hosts, Fox News Channel, and small-town Americans.

For a self-proclaimed man of the people, Barack Obama has

shown a remarkable lust for power. For a man who promised to be postpartisan, he has shown an unprecedented tendency to demean, ignore, and silence his opposition—from his White House website call for critics to be reported, to his insistence that his opponents just be quiet: "I will not waste time with those who have made the calculation that it's better politics to kill this plan than to improve it," he says. "I don't want the folks who created the mess to do a lot of talking. I want them just to get out of the way so [I] can clean up the mess."

Well, Mr. President, perhaps I can meet you halfway: When it comes to health care, let's just agree that *everyone* in the government should get out of the way.

FOUR

OBAMA THE APPEASER

From the beginning, it was clear that Barack Obama was part of the American left's "blame America first" crowd. He believed that America was hated around the world—and that it deserved all the criticism it received. Early on, he ingratiated himself with the left by becoming a major critic of George W. Bush's foreign policy. After all, he came with bona fide appeasement credentials: In a speech in October 2002, he declared his opposition to the invasion of Iraq.

During the 2008 campaign he harshly criticized President Bush for misallocating our resources toward the war on terror in Iraq, instead of directing everything toward Afghanistan, where Al Qaeda had trained for the 9/11 attacks. He portrayed our presence in Iraq as a distraction and a burden that actually diminished our security. "This war distracts us from every threat that we face and so many opportunities we could seize. By any measure, our single-minded and open-ended focus on Iraq is not a sound strategy for keeping Americans safe."[1] Obama carried his opposition to our effort in Iraq to another level when he opposed the surge crafted by General David Petraeus. Even long after the success of the strategy invalidated Obama's opposition, he refused to apologize—never, in his arrogance, willing to admit a mistake. And they said George W. Bush was stubborn!

Obama appeared obsessed with the slanderous notion that the only thing the American military was doing under George W. Bush was murdering innocent people in Afghanistan. "We've got to get the job done there and that requires us to have enough troops so that we're not just air-raiding villages and killing civilians, which is causing enormous pressure over there." [2] Like any liberal candidate who realizes his appeasement promotion won't sell well with the people, though, Obama was also determined to appear tough—always, of course, in the context of slamming Republicans. So while he criticized us for being too militaristic and imperialistic in Iraq, and brutish in Afghanistan, he promised that he'd go after Osama bin Laden and succeed where his predecessor had not. He said he'd send our troops into Pakistan to hunt him and other terrorists down, even without local permission. [3]

How's that pledge turned out, Mr. President?

Obama made clear that he favored diplomacy over militarism—leading the chorus of critics who scorned President Bush as a trigger-happy cowboy who fired his weapons first and worried about diplomacy later. He castigated Bush for his unilateralist approach to foreign policy—"the diplomacy of refusing to talk to other countries," he sniped [4]—and promised to "rebuild our alliances to take out terrorist networks." [5]

Obama campaigned as if he envisioned himself as president of the world, basking in the glow of rock star treatment in Europe when he spoke in Berlin to a crowd of two hundred thousand. Yet he never explained what he would have done differently to persuade unwilling nations to help the United States combat the threat of Saddam Hussein's Iraq, nor how he could have neutralized the corrupt alliances some of our European allies made with Saddam, which made it impossible to create an honorable consensus on how to eliminate the threat he posed to international stability.

As president-elect, Obama kept up his drumbeat of accommodation. He pledged a "new dawn of American leadership" that would be marked by an emphasis on diplomacy and multilateralism. No longer, he vowed, would America be the global bully. He trotted out Hillary Clinton, his secretary of state in waiting, to say, "We know our security, our values, and our interests cannot be protected and advanced by force alone nor, indeed, by Americans [alone]." The Obama presidency, she said, signaled a "new effort to renew America's standing in the world as a force for positive change."[6]

During the campaign, Obama had alarmed people by declaring that he would meet with enemy dictators, including Iran's Mahmoud Ahmadinejad, without preconditions—the only candidate to make such a foolish promise. His naïveté prompted ridicule from his primary rival, Hillary Clinton, who depicted Obama as inexperienced in foreign policy. "The American people don't have to guess whether I understand the issues or whether I'd have to rely on a foreign policy handbook," said Clinton. She needled him over his no-preconditions position, saying that she would "not pencil in" leaders of Iran, Venezuela, Cuba, and North Korea until their ambitions were assessed.[7] After Obama took a storm of criticism for his position, he subtly attempted to soften it, saying he hadn't meant that he wouldn't *prepare for* meetings. But the damage to his credibility was done.

While Obama instinctively blamed America for her poor standing in the world under President George W. Bush and promised to reverse that, he and his Democratic colleagues contributed to skepticism abroad by consistently characterizing the United States as a bad actor on the world stage. What did these liberals expect? Even if we'd been the world's favorite nation, their endless criticism as "insiders" would have turned favorable world opinion into disfavor.

Obama complained, for example, that Bush had alienated Muslims in the world—and yet a short time later, in a major foreign policy campaign speech, he made sure Muslims would resent us if they didn't already. He called our attack on Iraq "a misguided invasion of a Muslim country that sparks new insurgencies, ties down our military, busts our budgets, increases the pool of terrorist recruits, alienates America, gives democracy a bad name, and prompts the American people to question our engagement in the world."[8] He said that we had engaged in "a deliberate strategy to misrepresent 9/11 to sell a war against a country that had nothing to do with 9/11." Like other appeasement Democrats, he suggested that Bush had trumped up lies about Iraq's weapons of mass destruction because he "was determined to go to war."[9]

Obama used the favorite liberal cudgels of Guantanamo Bay and Abu Ghraib to beat Bush over the head. He told the world how terribly we had mistreated the poor innocent terrorists at Gitmo, and promised he would close the facility, reject the use of military commissions to try the prisoners, and adhere to the Geneva Conventions. He never backed up his charges with convincing evidence; nor did he bother explaining how Geneva applied to enemy combatants who didn't wear uniforms but slipped into civilian environments pretending not to be the enemy in order to wage their asymmetrical war.

Obama brought all his antiwar opportunism to exploit the

Abu Ghraib incident, despicably accusing the Bush administration of orchestrating the policies leading to the abuses, and thus of having adopted a deliberate policy of torture. He said, "As the counter-insurgency manual reminds us, we cannot win a war unless we maintain the high ground and keep the people on our side. But because the administration decided to take the low road, our troops have more enemies. Because the administration cast aside international norms that reflect American values, we are less able to promote our values." [10]

Obama never seemed happier than when he could lend his skills to running down his country.

WHOSE VALUES?

Obama always talked about restoring America's true values, but when he talked about those values he wasn't on the same page with most patriotic Americans I know. The priorities that seemed most important to him included treating our true enemies with kid gloves and apologizing for America's supposed imperialism. He obviously believed that America didn't deserve the wealth and prosperity she had earned, and that we had not been generous enough with our resources. In addition to projecting shame for America's special place in the world, his values would include protecting abortion on demand; confiscatory taxes to redistribute wealth; instinctive support for the world's brutal dictators; a disdain for capitalism; a belief that our courts should make laws and not just interpret them; a conviction that our courts should adopt the laws of other, more enlightened nations; an inclination to defer to international bodies; a belief that our federal government should be even more dominant over states; a determination to treat the war on terrorism more as a law enforcement matter than as a military one; and a feeling that people in rural America were warped for their strong faith and their belief in the right to bear arms.

APPEASEMENT POLICIES MATCH CAMPAIGN RHETORIC

During the campaign, some assumed that Obama was only talking like an appeaser to curry favor with his antiwar leftist base. Since he became president, however, I'm sorry to say that he has carried through on many of his promises. As one of his first official acts, he announced that he would close Gitmo, with no plans for where to relocate these hardened terrorists. Then, in February, he used his first address to a joint session of Congress to reiterate the theme he had articulated in announcing the closing of Gitmo—invoking the values meme again: "Living our values doesn't make us weaker. It makes us safer, and it makes us stronger." [11] Most realistic people understand that this is sheer psychobabble. Living Obama's values—appeasement squared— couldn't possibly make us safer. And it hasn't: Mere hours after Obama delivered his address, Iran began its first test run of a new nuclear reactor, built with Russian assistance. And by the end of 2009 we were seeing a marked increase in terrorist incidents, with two attempted airline attacks in the week of Christmas alone.

OBAMA'S WORLD APOLOGY TOUR

As much as Obama has dissed America while speaking to foreigners on foreign soil, it's amazing that he could accuse anyone else of damaging America's reputation in the international community. Indeed, anyone who doubted Obama's deep-seated resentment against this country couldn't credibly retain that skepticism after his extended world apology tour. He was obsessed with confessing America's flaws and correcting its course to atone for past sins.

Even before he was elected, Obama gave us a foretaste of what he'd do in office. In his July 2008 speech in Berlin, Obama said, "I know my country has not perfected itself. At times, we've struggled to keep the promise of liberty and equality for all of our people. We've made our share of mistakes, and there are times when our actions around the world have not always lived up to our best intentions." [12] And he kept up this practice after his inauguration. By the beginning of June, some estimated that he had apologized for America to nearly *three billion people* across Europe, the Americas, and the Muslim world. [13] In an interview with Al Arabiya on January 26, 2009—just days after taking office—he announced: "All too often the United States starts by dictating . . . and we don't always know all the factors that are involved. So let's listen. . . . And I think if we do that, then there's a possibility at least of achieving some breakthroughs. . . . My job to the Muslim world is to communicate that the Americans are not your enemy. We sometimes make mistakes. We have not been perfect." [14]

On March 25, Obama's secretary of state, Hillary Clinton, implicated the United States in the drug-related violence that has overrun Mexico. "I feel very strongly we have a co-responsibility" for the violence, she said. "Our insatiable demand for illegal drugs fuels the drug trade. Our inability to prevent weapons from being illegally smuggled across the border to arm these criminals causes the deaths of police officers, soldiers and civilians." [15]

And the apologies just kept coming:

- On April 1, in a press conference preceding the G20 meeting in London, Obama said, "If you look at the sources of this crisis, the United States certainly has some accounting to do with respect to a regulatory system that was inadequate." [16]

- On April 2, at the G20, Obama said, "I would like to think that with my election and the early decisions that we've made, that you're starting to see some restoration of America's standing in the world." He said on that day, "It is true, as my Italian friend has said, that the [economic] crisis began in the U.S. I take responsibility, even if I wasn't president at the time." [17] Big of him.

- On April 3, in Strasbourg, France, he said, "In America, there's a failure to appreciate Europe's leading role in the world. Instead of celebrating your dynamic union and seeking to partner with you to meet common challenges, there have been times where America has shown arrogance and been dismissive, even derisive." He did throw his fellow citizens a small bone, too: "But in Europe, there is an anti-Americanism that is at once casual but can also be insidious. Instead of recognizing the good that America so often does in the world, there have been times where Europeans choose to blame America for much of what's bad. On both sides of the Atlantic, these attitudes have become all too common." [18] I guess that's better than just slamming his own country, but you have to scratch your head at how casually he stereotypes— and condemns—most of the Western world.

- On April 5, in Prague, Obama declared, "As the only nuclear power to have used a nuclear weapon, the

United States has a moral responsibility to act" to reduce nuclear weapons.[19]

- On April 6, in Ankara, Turkey, he announced that "the United States is still working through some of our own darker periods in our history. . . . Our country still struggles with the legacies of slavery and segregation, the past treatment of native Americans." He said, "I know there have been difficulties these last few years. I know that the trust that binds us has been strained, and I know that strain is shared in many places where the Muslim faith is practiced. Let me say this as clearly as I can: the United States is not at war with Islam."[20] Well, he can pat himself all on the back all he wants for that breakthrough, but President Bush couldn't have been more explicit and clear in communicating precisely the same message. For Obama to imply otherwise undermined his stated purpose of proving how much we love the Muslim world. But I suppose sometimes his zeal to demonize President Bush overpowers even his urge to appease.

- On April 16, he wrote in an op-ed piece that was published in U.S. and Latin American newspapers before the Summit of the Americas: "Too often, the United States has not pursued and sustained engagement with our neighbors. We have been too easily distracted by other priorities and have failed to see that our own progress is tied directly to progress throughout the Americas. My administration is committed to renewing and sustaining a broader partnership between the United States and the hemisphere on behalf of our common prosperity and our common security."[21] If Obama truly believes we should engage more with Latin America, which he doubtless does, couldn't he have made the point without the gratuitous swipe at his own country—a swipe that validates, rather than diminishes, any negative perceptions Latin Americans might have?

• On April 18, in Port of Spain, Trinidad, for the summit, Obama said: "We have at times been disengaged, and at times we sought to dictate our terms. But I pledge to you that we seek an equal partnership. There is no senior partner and junior partner in our relations."[22]

At the summit, Obama sat through a fifty-minute anti-American harangue by Nicaraguan president Daniel Ortega, who condemned the United States for a century of what he described as imperialistic aggression. Obama didn't lift a finger to protest the tirade, much less defend his own country. Instead, in his egotistical manner, he said only that he was "grateful that President Ortega did not blame me for things that happened when I was three months old."[23]

Hugo Chavez gave Obama a copy of a book-length tract against America: *The Open Veins of Latin America: Five Centuries of Pillage of a Continent.* Its author, one Eduardo Galeano, described the United States as a "machine of killing peoples, devouring the world resources each day," and declared that "we are suffering a terrorist menace." Obama's response: "I think it was . . . a nice gesture to give me a book. I'm a reader."[24]

• On April 20, as he was rationalizing his dreadful decision to release Office of Legal Counsel memos detailing CIA enhanced interrogation techniques used against terrorist suspects, he said, "Don't be discouraged that we have to acknowledge potentially we've made some mistakes."[25]

- On May 21, at a speech at the National Archives in Washington, D.C., he trashed our prosecution of the war on terror: "There is also no question that Guantanamo set back the moral authority that is America's strongest currency in the world. Instead of building a durable framework for the struggle against al Qaeda that drew upon our deeply held values and traditions, our government was defending positions that undermined the rule of law." And he threw in another favorite argument of the antiwar left: "Indeed, the existence of Guantanamo likely created more terrorists around the world than it ever detained. So the record is clear: Rather than keeping us safer, the prison at Guantanamo has weakened American national security. It is a rallying cry for our enemies."[26] No, the rallying cry for our enemies is your mischaracterization of this prison—which is probably too luxurious, in fact, for the worst of the worst—and your policies of appeasement and retreat.

- Finally, at the National Archives, Obama said: "Unfortunately, faced with an uncertain threat, our government made a series of hasty decisions. . . . I also believe that all too often our government made decisions based on fear rather than foresight; that all too often our government trimmed facts and evidence to fit ideological predispositions. Instead of strategically applying our power and our principles, too often we set those principles aside as luxuries that we could no longer afford."[27]

Well, many of us don't agree with you, Mr. President. It seems to us that you, and your fellow leftists, are the ones who are hurting this country's position and security in the world—because your ideological predispositions prevent you from seeing real threats for what they are, and responding as the leader of a nation at war, not as some abject Father Confessor anxious to throw your own country under the bus.

WALKING SOFTLY WITH NO STICK

Sadly, America now has a sitting president who simply rejects the idea that America is a special place in the world. When asked in Europe if he believes in American exceptionalism, he gave another of his evasive, Clintonesque answers: "I believe in American exceptionalism. Just as the Brits believe in British exceptionalism and the Greeks in Greek exceptionalism." He just can't bring himself to say that America is exceptional—because he doesn't believe it. His mutliculturalist bent prevents him from seeing any culture as superior—or inferior, no matter how barbaric—to another. This is presumably why he inappropriately bowed to the Saudi king at the G20 summit in London in April, and then—presumably to make sure we all knew it wasn't a mistake—repeated the gesture in November, before Japan's Emperor Akihito.

It's difficult to imagine, but Obama is naïve and arrogant enough to believe that he alone has the ability to change America's image around the world—simply by running down the United States. Indeed, he and his crew seem to believe he's already succeeded. White House Press Secretary Robert Gibbs said early on that Obama's apologetic remarks to other nations had "changed the image of America around the world" and made the United

States "safer and stronger." As evidence, Gibbs pointed to the absence of protesters during the Summit of the Americas. But as Fox News contributor Karl Rove observed in a *Wall Street Journal* op-ed, it's foolish to judge a policy by the amount of protest it generates: "Ronald Reagan drew hundreds of thousands of protesters by deploying Pershing and cruise missiles in Europe. Those missiles helped win the Cold War."[28] Then again, Obama would have disagreed with that policy, too, wouldn't he? Otherwise, why would he have told Eastern European states that he was backing away from plans for an antimissile shield there on September 17—*the very anniversary of the Soviet invasion of Poland*? Is that how Obama believes he improves our standing in the world: by betraying our allies while snuggling up to our enemies?

With this little gesture, our grand master of diplomacy provoked a strong reaction from *Fakt*, a Polish tabloid daily with seven million readers. A piece in the paper headlined "Treason" began,

> Strategic ally? Mainstay of our security? End of illusions. The United States of America has turned his back to us. The U.S. president lightly tossed into the trash the anti-missile shield project in Poland and the Czech Republic. The massive military installation was to give special meaning to us in NATO and to strengthen our position towards Russia. But America prefers to work something out with Moscow instead of Warsaw. Yesterday the whole world went on about Barack Obama's decision. There will be no shield! The Kremlin triumphs, and the Poles have been exposed to the wind.[29]

Beyond damaging our image in the world in the name of enhancing it, there are other hazards involved when our president slams the United States on every acre of foreign soil he touches.

As Rove noted, "when a president desires personal popularity, he can lose focus on vital American interests. . . . The desire for popularity has led Mr. Obama to embrace bad policies,"[30] such as giving into European demands for crackdowns on tax havens and hedge funds, because he blamed us for the world financial crisis, and pushing for arms negotiations with Russia, because he feels it's our fault that our relationship with Russia "has been allowed to drift"—instead of dealing with America's real problems with Russia, such as its invasion of Georgia. Rove has it exactly right: "A superstar, not a statesman, today leads our country. That may win short-term applause from foreign audiences, but do little for what should be the chief policy preoccupation of any U.S. president: advancing America's long-term interests."

Indeed, despite all of Obama's groveling, the foreign leaders whose approval he craved have answered by rebuffing and even ridiculing him. Though Obama made repeated overtures to Cuba, Iran, North Korea, and Venezuela, after initially favorable responses they have responded largely by insulting him or rejecting his appeals for cooperation.

IRAN

Obama has shown his true foreign policy colors in his dealings with Iran. In his "Nowruz" (New Year's) greeting to the leaders of Iran, he referred to the country several times as "the Islamic Republic of Iran," which validated the standing of the theocratic leaders while offering a kick in the gut to the majority of Iranian people, who oppose them. When he called for "mutual respect" between our two nations, he demonstrated the moral bankruptcy of liberal moral equivalency positions on the world stage. How can he treat this brutal regime as if it deserves international respect?

In case anyone was laboring under the misimpression that Obama was just waxing diplomatic, and that his overtures didn't reflect his true feelings, he disabused them of that in his disgraceful reaction to Iranian president Mahmoud Ahmadinejad's election heist in June. As the Iranian people took to the streets by the thousands in protest—some were then brutally slaughtered by state forces—Obama held his tongue throughout the disgraceful ordeal, refusing to make solidarity with true democratic forces, saying that he wanted to withhold comment until there had been a thorough review. It was more than a week later before Obama would dare condemn the Iranian leadership— way too little, way too late. What did Obama get for his loyalty to the Iranian tyrant? Ahmadinejad lashed out at Obama for interfering in Iranian internal affairs and demanded an apology. As Mitt Romney noted, "It's very clear that the president's policies of going around the world and apologizing for America aren't working."[31]

Indeed, we're seeing the end result of Obama's appeasement approach with Iran—his "walk softly and carry no stick" posture. He issued a stern, unequivocal deadline that Iran must quit defying the world with her nuclear ambitions by the end of 2009. In May, after a meeting with Israeli prime minister Benjamin Netanyahu, he said, "the important thing is to make sure there is a clear timetable, at which point we say these talks don't seem to be making any clear progress."[32] But Ahmadinejad ignored Obama, bragging that he was "not intimidated" and was "10 times stronger than last year." In mid-December, he thumbed his nose at Obama's posture: "We don't care about international deadlines over Iran's nuclear program."[33]

When the deadline came and passed, Obama just brushed it off—just as he'd done with his Gitmo deadline, and his deadline to have health care passed "by August recess"—as if he'd never set the deadline in the first place. Secretary of State Hillary Clinton claimed that "we've avoided using the term 'deadline' ourselves. That's not a term that we have used because we want to keep the door to dialogue open." She might as well have said, "We really did set a deadline before, but we didn't mean it. Besides, we must accommodate Mahmoud, who will need more time to call us names."

As *Investor's Business Daily* has said, "The Iranian government is laughing and scoffing at America for our diplomatic naïveté and impotence. The Iranian people, yearning for freedom, see us as too cowardly or corrupt to help them—even with moral support. The American people see an administration that obviously doesn't mean what it tells its enemies." [34]

VENEZUELA, CUBA, NORTH KOREA, HONDURAS

Obama's magic has worked no better with Venezuelan dictator Hugo Chavez, who gave Obama the same treatment he gave George W. Bush. At the Copenhagen climate conference, Chavez said, "It still smells like sulfur in the world." He referred to Obama as the "Nobel Prize of War," for sending thirty thousand more troops to Afghanistan.

Cuban foreign minister Bruno Rodriguez insulted Obama about Copenhagen, calling him "imperial," "arrogant," and a liar. "He lies all the time, deceives with demagogic words, with profound cynicism." This followed harsh words from President Raul Castro and the December 5 arrest of an American citizen and contractor in Cuba.

And despite Obama's efforts to make nice with North Korean dictator Kim Jong Il—even writing him a personal letter—North

Korea returned the favor by demanding that UN sanctions be lifted, and praised the soldiers who kidnapped two U.S. journalists. Kim is reportedly planning on engaging in another nuclear test in 2010.[35]

Obama displayed his true colors when Honduran president Jose Manuel Zelaya attempted his unconstitutional power grab to abolish term limits and remain in office. When Zelaya couldn't muster the support of even his own legislative allies, and the nation's supreme court declared his actions unconstitutional, he sent his supporters—along with thugs loaned by Hugo Chavez and Daniel Ortega—to steal election ballots. At that point the nation's democratic forces had had enough and exiled him to Costa Rica.

Though Zelaya was the one guilty of subverting his nation's laws, Obama insisted on siding, once again, with the tyrant and against the true democratic forces. Hillary Clinton said that the Honduran forces ousting outlaw Zelaya "should be condemned by all." Obama, with an Orwellian flourish, said his administration would "stand with democracy" by supporting Zelaya's reinstatement. Obama's antidemocratic sympathies were consistent in his handling of both the Iranian and Honduran crises. What was inconsistent were his shameless, overt attempts to intervene in the internal affairs of Honduras even as he refused to lift a finger of protest with Iran, saying he wanted to respect Iranian sovereignty.

OVERSEAS CONTINGENCY OPERATIONS

President Obama subscribes to the leftist view that radical Muslim extremists resort to terrorism in large part because of their grievances against the United States and the West, and that some of these grievances are justified. As we've seen, he has condemned our pre-Obama foreign policy, our "war of choice" against Iraq, the torture and abuse charges against America (which he has trumped up), and the very existence of Gitmo prison, all as recruitment tools for terrorists—as if to say that jihadists wouldn't engage in jihad against America if those things hadn't occurred. During his first week in office he signed an executive order stating that Gitmo would be closed within a year. Regrettably, he's still trying to live up to that order, no matter what hazards it entails.

But that was just the beginning. Since that time he has embarked on a course that can only be described as unilaterally withdrawing from the war on terror, pretending it doesn't exist and that it will just go away if we decide not to participate. He has proceeded to downgrade our antiterror efforts from waging war to relying on law enforcement, which has had grave consequences for our national security. He has rejected the phrase "war on terror" and substituted the weakly generic "overseas contingency operations." His homeland security secretary, Janet Napolitano, abandoned the word *terrorism* in favor of "man-caused disaster," to avoid the "inflammatory" language of what she called the "politics of fear." Obama has ordered that captured terrorists be read Miranda "rights" on the battlefield, and he has reassigned terrorist interrogation duties from the CIA to an interagency entity operating out of the White House.

Obama has also selectively released documents describing our enhanced interrogation techniques into the public domain. Conspicuously absent from the document dump were records showing the lifesaving information the government gleaned from its interrogations. Even President Obama's CIA director, Leon Panetta, strongly objected to publicizing documents revealing our interrogation techniques. Not only would this decision reveal details of our interrogation methods to the terrorists, it would also risk compromising joint operations with our allies that have helped us in the past to capture terrorists.

Former vice president Dick Cheney has correctly criticized Obama for reversing the Bush administration's antiterrorism policies, saying that the decision to back off would make us more vulnerable. Last May, in a blistering speech at the American Enterprise Institute challenging Obama's appeasement policies, Cheney defended the Bush administration's approach to the war, saying that it had not engaged in torture and had only implemented policies necessary to keep the nation safe. He answered Obama's specious charge that we have betrayed our values in our conduct of the war: "Critics of our policies are given to lecturing on the theme of being consistent with American values. But no moral value held dear by the American people obliges public servants ever to sacrifice innocent lives to spare a captured terrorist from unpleasant things. And when an entire population is targeted by a terror network, nothing is more consistent with American values than to stop them."

Cheney set out in clear terms the philosophical differences between the two administrations in their approach to combating terrorism:

So we're left to draw one of two conclusions—and here is the great dividing line in our current debate over national security. You can look at the facts and conclude that the comprehensive strategy has worked, and therefore needs to be continued as vigilantly as ever. Or you can look at the same set of facts and conclude that 9/11 was a one-off event—coordinated, devastating, but also unique and not sufficient to justify a sustained wartime effort. Whichever conclusion you arrive at, it will shape your entire view of the last seven years, and of the policies necessary to protect America for years to come.[36]

It wasn't enough for Obama to reverse the Bush-era policies. Like a third-world dictator punishing his conquered predecessors, he decided to criminalize officials from the Bush administration. Despite the fact that the Justice Department had already conducted a nonpartisan, thorough review and concluded that there should be no prosecutions—that there was "insufficient evidence of criminal conduct, insufficient evidence of the subject's involvement; insufficient evidence of criminal intent; and low probability of conviction" on the part of CIA terrorist investigators—Obama confirmed his 9/10 mind-set and partisan vitriol when he affirmed his politicized Justice Department's decision to reinvestigate the matter.

Obama outdid himself, though, with the decision—which he claims was made exclusively by Attorney General Eric Holder— to bring 9/11 mastermind Khalid Sheikh Mohammed and four high-profile Al Qaeda terrorists to New York for trial in our civilian courts. *National Review*'s Andy McCarthy, who led the successful prosecution against the blind sheik Omar Abdel Rahman in the 1990s for the first World Trade Center attack, wrote, "The decision . . . is one of the most irresponsible ever made by a presidential administration. That it is motivated by politics could not be more obvious." The antiwar left, said McCarthy, which has always wanted to put the Bush administration on trial, will now get "its promised feast."

It later surfaced that Obama hadn't even conferred with New York officials about moving the trial to New York, or about the security implications involved.[37] His real purpose was to reverse course and show these mistreated jihadists that we could be wonderful people and thus deter them from future attacks against us.

It didn't take long for Obama's policies to bear fruit. As it turns out, Dick Cheney hadn't exaggerated in suggesting that Obama viewed 9/11 as a one-off event—and this view would have increasingly troubling implications. When a jihadist attempted to bring down Northwest Airlines flight 253 from Amsterdam to Detroit, Obama couldn't bring himself to identify the action as terrorism, instead calling the Nigerian attacker an "isolated extremist"—despite reports that the man had been trained in Yemen. It takes willful blindness or stupefying political correctness not to acknowledge this was part of the same international jihad.

Obama's absurd position was soon refuted—by Al Qaeda itself, which proudly claimed responsibility for the attack.[38] It came to light, via ABC News, that two of the men behind the bombing plot had been released from Guantanamo Bay and were now leaders of Al Qaeda in the Arabian Peninsula.[39] Worse yet, it appears that the U.S. government had intelligence from Yemen before the attempted bombing that Al Qaeda leaders there were talking about preparing "a Nigerian" for a terrorist attack.[40] Two federal officials reportedly told the *New York Times* that U.S. intelligence was aware that "a Nigerian Muslim" was preparing an attack, yet officials did nothing to give warning of such an attack. The United States did not even raise a terror alert. Despite Al Qaeda's threats to mount more attacks, the administration stubbornly refused to raise the threat level following the incident.[41]

Not only that, but true to form, the Obama administration decided to treat the attacker, Umar Farouk Abdulmutallab, as a criminal to be tried by the courts, rather than as an enemy combatant. As a result, he was read his Miranda "rights" after only fifty minutes of interrogation;[42] and experts estimated that much information that could have been extracted from him was forfeited in our misguided effort to be loved by the world. Former prosecutor Victoria Toensing wrote that it was wrong to compare the Bush administration's referral of shoe bomber Richard Reid to the civilian courts, because his attempted attack took place only three months after 9/11, when there was no military commission in place. As she pointed out, not only is there now a commission to handle such matters, but there is also "a precedent of trying a non-citizen terrorist, the legal farce of the trial of Zacarias Moussaoui, who tied the court up for years before pleading guilty." Toensing echoed the concerns of others about the administration's decision, which could seriously impede the interrogation process and hamper the acquisition of important information that could help to save lives.[43]

In light of this debacle with Abdulmutallab, the Obama administration's dreadful national security policies have been confirmed as a disaster in the making. McCarthy put it best: "Obama sold himself as the anti-Bush, argued in favor of the Clinton law-enforcement approach of the nineties, has difficulty acknowledging that we are at war, believes we should engage rather than challenge pro-jihadist regimes, and staffed his administration with many people (especially lawyers) who virulently opposed Bush-style counterterrorism. The Christmas '09 attack did not happen in the immediate aftermath of 9/11, and its occurrence blows gigantic holes in Obama's delusional claims that we can be safer by turning away from a law-of-war paradigm and 'changing the tone' with the Muslim world."[44]

PART II

Learning from History

FIVE

WHY I'M A REAGAN CONSERVATIVE

Liberals have a tendency to revise history to align with their worldview, retelling the past in a way that serves the advancement of their modern agenda. They do this with our distant past as a nation—from demonizing Columbus to downplaying the centrality of the Christian influence on our founding. They do it with more modern events, from their treatment of the Vietnam War to their convenient omission of their brethren's environmental hysteria over global cooling just three decades ago. And it may be no surprise that they've distorted no period of history more shamelessly than the Reagan years. By the time of Reagan's death, this period was recognized by clear-thinking observers as a showcase for the vindication of the conservative ideas the fortieth president championed throughout his life. Yet even today, against all evidence, liberals persist in painting it as the "Decade of Greed." Why? Because those years serve as a thorough, real-life repudiation of their ideology and their political prescriptions.

In recent years, liberals have also sanitized their demonization of Ronald Reagan the man. There are two main reasons, in my view, for this abrupt change of face. One is that Reagan has enjoyed a resurgence of popularity with the American people, and liberals don't want to appear too out of step with that trend. The other is that rewriting their record of open disdain for Reagan made their even worse treatment of George W. Bush appear more personal than ideological. It allowed them to shift the focus from their rejection of Bush's conservative policies—which so many Americans supported—to their complaints about his "swagger" and "stubbornness" and "ignorance." They would rather attack individuals like Bush and Cheney and Sarah Palin, now a Fox News contributor, for their personal attributes than to attack the successful and effective conservative policies those leaders have championed.

Today, I believe we're facing a crossroads in America's future—a choice between, on one hand, a disastrous path of socialism at home and weakness on the world stage, and on the other, free-market capitalism, moral authority, and steadfast security. In the upcoming elections, we will choose our path. And before we do, I believe we must remind ourselves of the example set by the most successful president in modern times—Ronald Reagan.

LIBERALS ENLIGHTENED, CONSERVATIVES SIMPLISTIC

Liberals have long posed as generous and open-minded, but their actions speak louder than their words: The truth is, they're the least tolerant group in our political universe. They abhor conservatives, much as they disdain or condescend to hardworking average Americans. And their dislike often comes from a very personal place. They're convinced that conservatives are unenlightened, ignorant, and morally deficient. Their depiction of George W. Bush as an unsophisticated dolt, and of Sarah Palin as shallow, were hardly new developments: Decades before they started mining the comic potential of "Bushisms"—their perception that Bush butchered the English language—they were describing Ronald Reagan an "amiable dunce," a "California cowboy" who fell asleep at cabinet meetings and couldn't engage in complex thought even if his life, or the nation's well-being, depended on it. (Yet they cut Obama enormous slack every time he made a gaffe—remember when he claimed he'd campaigned in "fifty-seven states"?[1])

By contrast, they regard liberal politicians as brilliant. Remember how they fawned over Jimmy Carter's intelligence and erudition, even after he'd proven his inability to govern his way out of a paper bag? Today, of course, Reagan is recognized as the Great Communicator, as a prolific and brilliant writer—and as the man who lifted America out of the malaise of the Carter era.

The left may wax complimentary today about Ronald Reagan's personal attributes. But don't believe them for a minute: They were vicious toward him when it really mattered. They can rewrite their history of the modern era to hide their nastiness, but they can't change the facts. The same holds true today: Liberals tend to regard conservatives not only as unenlightened, but potentially dangerous—as with the Obama administration's characterization of Tea Party protesters as domestic terrorists. They couldn't have been happier than when they were condemning George W. Bush as a trigger-happy hawk: The *Boston Globe* called his designation of the Axis of Evil "a gratuitous blunder,"[2] and Jimmy Carter called it "overly simplistic and counterproductive."[3] A chorus of leftist voices piled on.

And the liberal U.S. press doted on every disapproving comment from overseas. *Newsweek* wrung its hands over the foreign reception to Bush's Axis of Evil, reporting that the French described it as "alarmist," the Australians as "worryingly simplistic and selective." One English source said, "many outside America are likely to find [his views] distinctly disturbing."[4] When Bush visited Japan in early 2002, the *Los Angeles Times* reported that the press there had "dogged" him for his Axis of Evil speech. "For many Japanese," they said, "Bush's good-versus-evil language is unsettling . . . as the product of a worldview that sees black and white but doesn't always seem to appreciate the area in between where most people live."[5] Three cheers for moral relativism disguised as liberal tolerance and compassion!

Salon's David Talbot said that Bush's black-and-white rhetoric reflected his failure to comprehend the world's complexity. "Bush utters the word 'evil' the way a child does when it first dawns on him that there is darkness and danger in the world, and only his goodness and courage stand in its way. . . . It simply confuses the American public and underlines what a dismal imitation of a great president our current leader is."[6]

But liberal revulsion at Bush's willingness to recognize good and evil forces in the world was nothing new for them. It's been part and parcel of their worldview since the days of Ronald Reagan, whom they feared even more. Decades before Bush called out North Korea, Iraq, and Iran as evil regimes and described Islamic terrorists as "evildoers," it was Ronald Reagan—to the horror of liberals everywhere—who reintroduced moral considerations into American foreign policy by depicting the Soviet Union as an "evil empire" and "the focus of evil in the modern world."

Reagan first invoked the term in a speech to the National Association of Evangelicals in Orlando, Florida, on March 8, 1983. Liberals came unglued after the speech, calling Reagan a warmonger—which recalled Soviet tyrant Joseph Stalin's calling Winston Churchill a Hitler-like warmonger when he declared that "an Iron Curtain [had] descended across the Continent."

Liberals were mortified with Reagan, whom they considered

another warmonger with a "button problem."[7] Columnist Tom Wicker warned that

> the greater danger lies in Reagan's vision of the superpower relationship as good versus evil, and his near-proclamation of holy war against 'an evil empire.' . . . If the president of the United States proclaims to the world the view that this country's relationship with the Soviet Union is a death struggle with evil, then his own words inevitably suggest that there can be no real compromise with that evil—not on arms control or anything else. . . . Why should those proclaimed as the "focus of evil" believe in the possibility of real compromise with a United States dedicated to their destruction?[8]

It must not have occurred to Wicker that the Soviet Union, by its own express statements, was dedicated to *our* destruction. So was compromise with them impossible? Well, Reagan *did* compromise with them—despite liberal skepticism—but he did so from a position of strength, based on an awareness that they were enemies who had threatened to "bury" us, and that we had to regard them as such, not soft-pedal them. Similarly, President George W. Bush recognized we are in a war with radical Islamists; President Obama believes we can make nice with the jihadists and treat our death struggle against them as a law enforcement matter rather than the prosecution of a war.

In addition to believing that U.S. policy serves as recruitment fodder for terrorists, Obama subscribes to the misguided liberal view that terrorism is also born of poverty around the world— a classic socialist, economic-determinist worldview. This is yet another case where liberals don't allow the facts to cloud their judgment: Study after study has shown that the idea that poverty

leads to terrorism is hogwash.[9] Poverty no more causes terrorism than prosperity cures it—as the example of the millionaire
Osama bin Laden demonstrates. A recent study confirms that
"individuals who support and commit terrorist acts are likely to
be more highly educated and have higher incomes than others
in their society."[10] The terrorists hate us not because they are
materially poor, but because of their wicked ideology. The more
we fail to recognize this, the more our difficulties in fighting
terrorism are increased.

The liberal reaction to Reagan and Bush goes beyond horror
at these conservative presidents' alleged appetite for war. We've
seen how liberals of the 1980s dismissed Ronald Reagan as "simplistic," in the same way as modern liberals dismissed George W.
Bush. After Reagan's Evil Empire speech, Anthony Lewis of the
New York Times huffed that "the real Ronald Reagan was speaking in Orlando. The exaggeration and the simplicities are there
not only in the rhetoric but in the process by which he makes
decisions."[11]

But those who scorned Reagan at the time have long since
been proven wrong. It was the vision, the foresight, the steadfast
adherence to principle, and above all the leadership of Ronald
Reagan that ended the Cold War and helped usher in a new era
of prosperity at home. His vision is as relevant today as it was in
his time. And if we lose sight of it—as we're in danger of doing
now—it will be at our peril.

I'm proud to call myself a Reagan conservative. I firmly believe in American exceptionalism, in limited government, and in
maximizing our individual liberties. I wholeheartedly subscribe
to Ronald Reagan's view that America is not the cause of corruption and evil abroad, but rather the cure for it.

On foreign policy I believe in peace through strength—in

maintaining the strongest military in the world and adapting our defenses and intelligence capabilities to the modern threats we face in the war on terror. On domestic policy, I'm a supply-sider on taxes and believe we should drastically cut government spending. And on social policy, I believe we should protect the life of the unborn and the institution of traditional marriage.

Though contemporary critics derided Reagan's views as simplistic and dangerous, time has shown that his big-picture approach to government—emphasizing the "three-legged stool" of a strong defense, a strong economy, and strong social values—was both powerful and prudent. He believed, as I do, that freedom is a God-given right, and that government should not regulate or control every aspect of our lives.

Those principles have never been more timely than they are today.

PEACE THROUGH STRENGTH

Long before he became president, Reagan was well aware that many viewed his strong stand on national security as unnecessarily antagonistic. In one of the most important political speeches in modern times—a 1964 campaign speech for Barry Goldwater, entitled "A Time for Choosing"—he made a powerful statement of his views:

> Those who would trade our freedom for the soup kitchen of the welfare state have told us that they have a utopian solution of peace without victory. They call their policy "accommodation." And they say if we only avoid any direct confrontation with the enemy, he will forget his evil ways and learn to love us. All who oppose them are indicted as warmongers. They say

we offer simple answers to complex problems. Well, perhaps there is a simple answer—not an easy answer—but simple: If you and I have the courage to tell our elected officials that we want our national policy based upon what we know in our hearts is morally right.

We cannot buy our security, our freedom from the threat of the bomb, by committing an immorality so great as saying to a billion now in slavery behind the Iron Curtain, "Give up your dreams of freedom because to save our own skin, we are willing to make a deal with your slave masters." . . . Let's set the record straight. There is no argument over the choice between peace and war, but there is only one guaranteed way you can have peace—and you can have it in the next second— surrender. . . .

There's a risk in any course we follow . . . but every lesson in history tells us that the greater risk lies in appeasement, and this is the specter our well-meaning liberal friends refuse to face—that their policy of accommodation is appeasement, and it gives no choice between peace and war, only between fight and surrender. If we continue to accommodate, continue to back and retreat, eventually we have to face the final demand—the ultimatum. . . .

Khrushchev has told his people [that] when the time comes to deliver the final ultimatum, our surrender will be voluntary, because by that time we will have weakened from within spiritually, morally, and economically. He believes this because from our side he has heard voices pleading for "peace at any price" . . . And therein lies the road to war, because those voices don't speak for the rest of us. . . .

You and I have the courage to say to our enemies, *There is a price we will not pay. There is a point beyond which they must not advance.* This is the meaning in the phrase of Barry Goldwater's, "Peace through strength." [12]

Reagan's words deserve careful attention from anyone weighing the choices before us today. He might as well have been talking to George W. Bush's critics when he said, "They say we offer simple answers to complex problems. Well, perhaps there is a simple answer—not an easy answer—but simple. . . . You and I have the courage to say to our enemies, *There is a price we will not pay.*" And he might as well have been talking to Barack Obama when he said, "they say if we only avoid any direct confrontation with the enemy, he will forget his evil ways and learn to love us. . . . Every lesson in history tells us that the greater risk lies in appeasement, and this is the specter our well-meaning liberal friends refuse to face—that their policy of accommodation is appeasement, and it gives no choice between peace and war, only between fight and surrender."

If Barack Obama could only absorb Reagan's message and apply it to America's dealings with our enemies today. We must not delude ourselves into believing that the Islamic jihadists, like the communists of Reagan's era, will put down their swords if we simply accommodate their demands in the Middle East or elsewhere. They will not be swayed by our attempts to reach out to the Muslim world. (After all, they have their own complaints with other Muslims throughout the world.) They will not discontinue their suicide bombings—regardless of whether we close Gitmo, hold show trials of terrorists near Ground Zero in New York City, beat ourselves up over enhanced interrogations, or continue to treat terrorists as mere criminal defendants and not enemy combatants. This approach couldn't be more dangerous and more counterproductive to our peace and security.

"MR. GORBACHEV, TEAR DOWN THIS WALL"

Reagan displayed his focus and resolve when he set his sights on defeating the Soviet Union in the Cold War. Instead of settling for an endless stalemate, he was determined to rebuild our military and treat the new Soviet leader, Mikhail Gorbachev, as an adversary, not as our best friend. Reagan's critics complained that he was escalating hostilities between our two countries, accelerating the arms race and risking another World War. But Reagan was convinced that the path to peace was through building up our military and economic strength.

When feckless liberals, including the members of the global "peace movement," frantically pushed the United States to adopt a Nuclear Freeze policy in the late 1970s and early '80s, Reagan understood that this would be suicidal for the United States. He knew that the deceitful Soviet communist regime would lull us into ending our nuclear program while they continued theirs unabated. That's why he subscribed to the policy of "trust but verify," which was designed to preclude any such Soviet chicanery.

When the Soviets deployed SS-20 missiles (two-stage, intermediate-range missiles, many of them mobile and hard to track, and most aimed at our European allies), Reagan approved NATO's deployment of Pershing II missiles in West Germany, which sent appeasement liberals into hysteria. But Reagan wasn't going to continue the recent pattern of retreat in response to Soviet aggression, which had always invited further aggression.

Reagan outsmarted and outlasted Gorbachev, who balked when Reagan insisted on pursuing his vision of a Strategic Defense Initiative (SDI) at the Geneva summit in 1985. The proposed missile defense system—decried as "Star Wars" by liberals—became a pivotal issue at the leaders' summit in Reykjavik, Iceland, the following year, where Reagan famously walked out after Gorbachev refused to negotiate unless Reagan agreed to abandon SDI. In their third summit, however, Gorbachev caved and Reagan prevailed—not just because of Reagan's negotiating skills, but also because by then Reagan had turned the United States into an economic and military powerhouse once again while Gorbachev's economic reforms were failing.

Nor did Reagan reduce his pressure on Gorbachev after that astounding victory. On June 12, 1987, while attending a 750th anniversary celebration for the city of Berlin, Reagan stood before the Brandenburg Gate and challenged Gorbachev to tear down the Berlin Wall—a demand that symbolized not just the destruction of a physical barrier between freedom and slavery, but the end to Soviet communist oppression. In short order, Reagan's policies and pressure would bear fruit: The wall did come down, and the entire Soviet empire disintegrated soon thereafter.

The lesson here is simple. When conservatives defend the principle of peace through strength, they needn't resort to mere academic theories. The record of history is all they need.

A RISING TIDE LIFTS ALL BOATS

Reagan also demonstrated his resolve when he embarked on a singular path to rescue his country from an era of malaise, pessimism, stagnation, and stagflation—offering further lessons that should be heeded by any responsible politician today.

When Ronald Reagan took office, the liberal darling Jimmy Carter left him a nation in economic shambles: 7.4 percent unemployment heading toward 10 percent; double-digit inflation;

and interest rates of some 21 percent.[13] The country needed help, and fast.

Reagan responded by making broad supply-side cuts in marginal income tax rates, designed to break the logjam in the American economy. Liberals were up in arms at the cuts, crying that they would send federal revenues plummeting. They painted Reagan as a reverse Robin Hood, stealing from the poor and giving to the rich, while causing unmanageable budget deficits.

The opposite is true. After Reagan's tax cuts, the rich actually paid *more* taxes, proportionately, than they had before the cuts were implemented. A 1990 Bureau of Census report showed that the plight of all income groups, from poor to wealthy, improved during Reagan's time in office. A staggering 86 percent of people in the lowest fifth of income earners moved into higher income groups in the Reagan decade. During this period, the United States experienced unprecedented peacetime economic growth, with some twenty million new jobs, negligible inflation, and reduced interest rates—combinations most economics experts said couldn't be done. Real after-tax income per person rose by 15.5 percent, and real median income of families, before taxes, went up 12.5 percent.[14]

While it's true that deficits did increase during the Reagan years, there are misconceptions about why, and it's important to understand the difference between the real economic reasons for the increase and the liberals' efforts to blame it on Reagan. The deficit *did not* increase because Reagan's tax cuts reduced revenues—one of the most pernicious Democratic myths of the last twenty-five years. In fact, revenues *increased* dramatically during the 1980s, nearly doubling (nominal federal revenues grew from $517 billion to more than $1 trillion and, in constant inflation-adjusted dollars, revenues increased by 28 percent).[15]

Federal spending did jump, but in large part the increases were due to Reagan's deliberate and necessary increases in defense spending, which doubled during the decade. Still, even with a mostly recalcitrant Congress during many of those years, domestic spending grew more slowly under Reagan than under his predecessors; it actually fell as a percentage of GDP. Finally, it's often overlooked that Reagan's deficits decreased substantially toward the end of his second term; though liberals had threatened that the economy would collapse under their weight, their fears proved unfounded.[16]

THE DEATH OF THE THREE-LEGGED STOOL?

It's only natural for liberals to oppose Reagan's three-legged stool; it's their job. But it's interesting that they aren't as strident about it as elections approach, because they know—from their internal polling, if nothing else—that this is still a center-right nation. Pay attention, and you'll see what I mean: You'll never get a liberal to own up to his liberalism anywhere close to the month of November in even years. They all pretend to want to reduce taxes "for working folks," and even to be fiscal hawks. They tout themselves as strong on national defense and swear they adore the military. They profess that they personally oppose abortion, yet insist they can't impose their personal preference on women, whose "right to choose" to terminate their unborn babies' lives on demand merits the highest protection.

As soon as the election results are in, of course, they relapse into their addictions to various liberal policies, including increases on everything from ordinary income taxes to capital gains taxes, estate taxes, corporate taxes, luxury taxes, windfall profits taxes, cap-and-trade taxes, health-care taxes, tobacco taxes, junk food taxes, and so on and so on. From there they march out their parade of misguided "progressive" ideas—policies that would undermine our national defense, decimate our intelligence capabilities, and make abortion freely accessible under any circumstances.

Given the overwhelmingly liberal bias of the mainstream media, it's not surprising how often we hear about how "antiquated" Reagan conservatism is. But then the media never liked Reagan or his policies in the first place. They always demeaned social conservatism as the product of mean-spirited and uncompassionate Christian conservatives who are opposed to welfare and want to legislate their morality on the issues of abortion and homosexual marriage. On national defense, as we've seen, they've tarred conservatives as militarists, imperialists, warmongers, unilateralists, and American chauvinists who thumb their noses at the international community. On taxes, they ridiculed the right as greedy and favoring the wealthy to the detriment of fiscal responsibility.

One of their favorite lines of attack was that you can't cut taxes, raise defense spending, and balance the budget all at the same time. But in fact you *can* do just that—if not for other wasteful and counterproductive government programs that are far less justified under our constitutional scheme than necessary defense expenditures. Of course, Reagan wouldn't have been obliged to "raise" defense spending so drastically if Jimmy Carter hadn't cut the military so severely. But he did. Thankfully, our economy, due to the robust growth generated by the Reagan tax cuts, was able to absorb those necessary expenditures.

The key fact to recognize, however, is that supply-side tax cuts have never been inconsistent with balancing the budget—not in the Kennedy years, the Reagan years, or the George W.

Bush years. Liberals have simply used the mainstream media echo chamber to characterize tax cuts as irresponsible—just as they use it to portray conservatism as a harsh, uncompassionate, ineffective fringe ideology. The rest of the nation, they say, is moderate, even receptive to "progressive" ideas.

But don't believe it. Whenever the American people take a hard look at some new "progressive" idea—whether it's Hillary-care or Obamacare, cap-and-trade, or wasteful "stimulus" bills, they see through it every time.

THE PROVERBIAL "BIG TENT"

We hear a constant drumbeat today—in the liberal media and in some reputedly conservative circles—that Republicans should moderate their approach in order to appeal to centrists and in-dependents. You can't fill a big tent, they say, by sticking to firm conservative principles, which they condemn as extremist and polarizing. In the 1970s and '80s, some Republicans said the same thing in criticizing Ronald Reagan, cautioning against his "strident" rhetoric and his uncompromising approach on social issues, particularly abortion. But how do you compromise when it comes to the life of the most innocent among us? As Reagan biographer Paul Kengor wrote, "Abortion was a moral issue on which [Reagan] refused to compromise as president. He un-derstood what pro-choice Republicans do not: Abortion is the preeminent moral problem of our time." [17] He went so far as to compare abortion with slavery:

> This nation fought a terrible war so that black Americans would be guaranteed their God-given rights. Abraham Lin-coln recognized that we could not survive as a free land when

some could decide whether others should be free or slaves. Well, today another question begs to be asked: How can we survive as a free nation when some decide that others are not fit to live and should be done away with?

I believe no challenge is more important to the character of America than restoring the right to life to all human beings. Without that right, no other rights have meaning.[18]

Reagan felt strongly that the best path forward for Republicans must involve a rigorous adherence to conservative principles, not a softening of their resolve or a dilution of their core convictions in the service of compromise. As he told conservatives in his CPAC speech, the new party he envisioned could not be limited to "country club–big business" Republicans; it must have room for factory workers, farmers, cops, and other who had never considered joining the party before, but who shared the conservative values it stood for. Reagan sought to win back the social conservatives the Democratic Party had turned its back on during the 1960s. He believed that these new constituencies were not just to be exploited for their votes, as Democrats have always done, but enlisted to serve as party leaders and candidates.

Reagan was passionate about this. He had no desire to carve out a narrow niche for rigid, hard-boiled conservatism, an extremist stance that would alienate the masses. On the contrary, he believed that, by clearly laying out his commonsense principles, he could attract the widest grouping of Americans to this "new" Republican Party *without* compromising fundamental principles. His electoral landslides validated his belief that mainstream America did, in fact, share his conservative values—and modern polls continue to speak to the timelessness of his approach. In September 2009, and again in January 2010, Gallup reported that twice as many Americans identify themselves as conservative as liberal.[19]

COUNTRY CLUB REPUBLICANS

Republicans have always had, among their ranks, a certain number who claim to be "mainstream," even conservative, but whose views and attitudes are so moderate as to be out of step with true conservatives. Whether you call them country club Republicans, Beltway elitists, northeastern "progressive Republicans," or just Republicans in name only (RINOs), they have always expressed their disapproval—even contempt—for many of the principles of Reagan conservatism, and for real conservative Republicans themselves. They look down their noses on authentic conservatives, especially those who don't measure up to their blue-blood requirements for pedigree, such as Sarah Palin. A recent poll of GOP insiders bears this out, revealing that these elitists—the ones who insisted on nominating John McCain, my friend but certainly a centrist—in no way support Governor Palin.[20]

These Beltway types often obstruct true conservative reform—as they did with the Republicans' 1994 Contract with America, as former House majority leader Dick Armey has attested. Along with Newt Gingrich, Armey was instrumental in crafting and implementing the Contract and the "Republican Revolution" it helped to usher in, countering leftist excesses dating back to LBJ and arguably FDR, and helping lead the way to George W. Bush's election in 2000.[21]

Most of these "centrists" are pro-abortion but see themselves as fiscal and national defense conservatives. But they differ from mainstream conservatives on some fiscal issues as well, being stuck in a time warp on tax policy, believing the liberal myth that taxes and revenue follow a zero-sum pattern: that you can't reduce tax rates without reducing revenues, despite historical evidence to the contrary.

The elitists in our party will always look down on the conservative everyman, who insists on adhering to values grounded in moral absolutes. And they usually agree with liberals that Republicans must "moderate" their positions to be successful. Each group, though, has different motives for urging conservative moderation. Liberals are hardly interested in promoting the GOP's best interests. Sabotage is more like what they have in mind. As they instinctively know that diluted conservatism doesn't sell as well with the electorate, they urge moderation. The country clubbers, on the other hand, are interested in making the GOP more liberal, because *they're* more liberal, especially on social issues. But the idea both groups share—that moving to the center will help Republicans attract Independents—is not based on reality. They can't point to any real evidence that the Republican Party will lose support from so-called independents by resisting the pull to the center. Indeed, the Reagan record shows the opposite—as do recent trends I'll discuss in Part III.

So the next time you hear that we Republicans can't win elections without moving to the center, remember who's putting out that message and what their respective motives are. The true key to conservative victory is to stay true to conservative principles; to convey the message clearly and powerfully; and to refuse to let liberals distort what we stand for and what is in our hearts.

FEE FI FO FRUM

In recent years, another group of naysayers has emerged to challenge these Republican principles—a splinter group represented by figures such as writer David Frum, George W. Bush's former aide and speechwriter. These figures claim to be both Republican and conservative, but in the end they are self-serving attention-seekers desperately trying to be loved by the mainstream media. They mistakenly believe that the time has passed for traditional Reagan conservatism and that we need to adapt the movement to meet the changing times. They contend that mainstream conservatism fails to recognize, or acknowledge, that we've all grown used to big government and must devise policies that accommodate the new big-government reality while still achieving somewhat conservative ends. These voices would have us capitulate to the inevitability of big government, embrace the prospect of an active, "energetic" federal government, and creatively design government programs that will appeal to the bulk of American voters. In other words, if you can't beat 'em, join 'em.

I believe this position is wrongheaded, cynically pragmatic, and ultimately destructive to our first principles and the time-less ends of American constitutional governance. On the issue of abortion, for example, Frum argues that Republicans should be less rigid in their approach to the problem, putting more emphasis on education and persuasion than on trying to make changes in law and public policy. (I personally think he presents us with a false choice: The pro-life movement has made consistent strides in persuading doubters, even as it engages in political activism to lobby for stricter abortion laws and the appointment of originalist judges. Their political advocacy has not precluded them from convincing increasing numbers of Americans—as polls indicate.)

Frum thinks that if Democrats play it right they'll wind up adopting a position that "two-thirds of American voters" support: "an emergency option available to adult women in dire need, provided that local majorities do not object too much." Republicans, he cautions, must not attempt "through the political process to shrink the abortion right beyond that point," because it could "call forth a pro-choice backlash in exactly the same way that *Roe v. Wade* summoned up the pro-life movement."[22]

I try to guard against the kind of rigid inflexibility that can tend to harden the most extreme political positions to the point of irrelevancy. But I certainly can't, in good conscience, make a raw political calculation about protecting the lives of the innocent unborn as casually as if we were talking about a no-smoking ban in a restaurant. We must continue to press for restrictions on abortion (such as parental notification) while striving for the appointment of Constitution-respecting judges *and* continuing our nonpolitical efforts to persuade Americans of the horrors and immorality of abortion.

I also reject Frum's premise that conservatives could trigger a backlash by sticking to our principles on this issue. With abortion, as with so many other political, social, and moral issues of our day, we must exercise leadership and set an example—and you don't set a worthy example by diluting your principles, especially in matters of life and death. I also strongly object to Frum's qualified prediction that Democrats will end up owning this issue. The reality is that Democrats aren't tempering *their* extremism on abortion; they only pretend to when it suits their immediate purposes. They are adamantly, militantly pro-abortion, to the point where even the very leader of their party, Barack Obama, as an Illinois senator in 2002, spoke out and voted against the Induced Infant Liability Act, which would have protected babies that survived late-term abortions.[23] Obama masquerades as a man of moderation and compromise when he speaks in generally pro-life venues, such as Notre Dame University. But he is doing everything he can to advance the cause of abortion—not choice, but unqualified abortion on demand—including deceitfully supporting and enabling the federal funding of abortion in the health-care bills that have circulated through Congress in the past year. As usual, it's the Democrats, not the Republicans, who are the extremists on this issue; conservatives need to do a better job of making that point.

There are many other areas of policy on which I disagree with Frum and other so-called "big-government conservatives" (an oxymoron if there ever was one). But my main philosophical difference with them is that I don't believe that the arrival of modern times requires us to abandon timeless principles.

Indeed, on closer inspection, it seems clear that the purveyors of this new brand of conservativism are receptive to abandoning, modifying, or diluting traditionally conservative principles, primarily because they don't believe in them to the extent mainstream conservatives do. For them, there are few conservative hills to die on.

Frum let the cat out of the bag on that score in the opening page of his chapter on life in his book *Comeback: Conservatism That Can Win Again*, where he confessed that he wasn't overly troubled by the hypothetical case of an abortion by a teenage girl from a low-income, single-parent family. Any of us might be sympathetic to such a young girl's circumstances, but those circumstances don't alter, one iota, the value of the human life she is carrying. If Frum were truly pro-life, he could not be as casually pragmatic as he seems to be in his approach to the abortion issue.

In my view, the logical conclusion—and, if widely adopted, the destiny—of Frumism is a surrender to liberalism, through the slow abandonment of core principles and the ceding of political turf. When we let liberals define the terms and venue of the debate, we guarantee our defeat. And that is the irony of Frum's "pragmatic conservatism": In the end, it's anything but pragmatic. If the conservative movement should adopt his approach to its defining issues, it would soon find itself in the worst of all worlds: losing both its political grounding and its moral authority.

STARS ALIGNING

Let not your hearts be troubled, though, for despite the presence of the Frums in our midst, the time is right for a resurgence of traditional conservatism. The recent excesses of Barack Obama and his Democratic Congress have shown the nation the dark and dangerous side of unchecked liberalism and how destructive it is for our nation.

Now is not the time for halfhearted commitment to our principles. Now is not the time to hold back in our clear presentation of conservative ideas, lest we be perceived as too strident, too extreme, or too polarizing. We must quit being gun-shy, as if we too were victims of liberal propaganda. I'm not saying we should be shrill. On the contrary, I'm saying that mainstream conservatism is neither harsh nor uncompassionate. Nor is it polarizing, for conservative positions are based firmly in American values. Liberals may try to polarize the country by distorting our position and exploiting these distortions in the form of class and race warfare, but we have the best weapon at hand to combat their efforts: the truth. If we communicate our views with confidence, the American people will recognize them as moral, compassionate, and in the best interests of this nation and its people.

SIX

OUR MODEL FOR UNITY AND ACTION: THE CONTRACT WITH AMERICA

Ronald Reagan is not the only model for successful conservative action in modern times. The more recent example of the Contract with America, a declaration "aimed at restoring the faith and trust of the American people in their government," shows us all how to translate conservative principles into action.

The Contract, which Newt Gingrich—now a Fox News contributor—introduced during the 1994 election cycle, was brilliant on many levels—not least because it empowered Republicans to nationalize congressional elections and communicate their message in a unified voice. "Nationalize" is no exaggeration: Some 367 Republican candidates for the House of Representatives signed the document and based their campaigns on its specific provisions. Not only that, but they put their money where their mouths were, publicly declaring, "If we break this Contract, throw us out." Some of this spirit inevitably bled over into Senate campaigns as well.

Dick Armey, another coauthor of the Contract, reminded us

that this goal of "nationalization" went beyond just winning the election. "What the Contract with America really did," wrote Armey, "was establish a national (as opposed to a parochial) vision for the Republican Party. When we took control, that positive Reagan vision of limited government and individual responsibility provided a great deal of discipline and allowed us to govern accordingly."[1] For me, that's one of the Contract's most important lessons: Republicans are most successful when they stick to their conservative principles—when they act affirmatively on their beliefs, rather than resigning themselves to a purely defensive game. When we have a clear sense of who we are and what we believe and are willing to apply our principles to governance—instead of forgetting who we are once we're in power—the changes we want will more readily fall into place. We would do well to remember that as we go forward with our new vision.

The Contract was bold, undertaking the ambitious task of reversing the growth of the central government that had been ongoing since FDR's New Deal in 1933. Conservatives had begun making headway in challenging this runaway statism in the 1960s with the ascendance of Barry Goldwater and conservative control of the GOP. Even with Goldwater's defeat and further setbacks in the 1970s, conservatives finally prevailed with the election of Ronald Reagan in 1980, which ushered in the Reagan Revolution. But as much as Reagan did to popularize conservative ideas, restore our national defenses, and reduce marginal tax rates to spur enormous economic growth, without a friendly Congress he was unable to reduce the size and scope of federal government activities. The ever-expanding bureaucracies continued to grow under his watch, as liberal Congresses thwarted his reform efforts. For real reform to take place, Republicans had to capture control of Congress, where laws are made—and others modified or repealed.

The Contract with America, then, carried on the unfinished business begun by Barry Goldwater and continued by Ronald Reagan. At last it gave conservatives an occasion to focus their efforts to decentralize government and shift power back to the states and local communities, as well as to the private sector.[2]

The Contract was the brainchild of Newt Gingrich, working with his fellow aggressive and innovative congressmen and a network of conservative think tanks, including the Heritage Foundation, to develop and shape the ideas that would find their way into the final document.

The Contract promised that, on the first day of the 104th Congress, the new Republican majority would immediately pass eight specific reforms:

FIRST, require all laws that apply to the rest of the country also apply equally to the Congress;

SECOND, select a major, independent auditing firm to conduct a comprehensive audit of Congress for waste, fraud or abuse;

THIRD, cut the number of House committees, and cut committee staff by one-third;

FOURTH, limit the terms of all committee chairs;

FIFTH, ban the casting of proxy votes in committee;

SIXTH, require committee meetings to be open to the public;

SEVENTH, require a three-fifths majority vote to pass a tax increase;

EIGHTH, guarantee an honest accounting of our Federal Budget by implementing zero base-line budgeting.

The Contract also pledged that, within the first hundred days of the 104th Congress, the new Republican majority would bring to the House floor ten bills, "each to be given full and open debate, each to be given a clear and fair vote and each to be immediately available this day for public inspection and scrutiny." The bills were:

THE FISCAL RESPONSIBILITY ACT: A balanced budget/tax limitation amendment and a legislative line-item veto to restore fiscal responsibility to an out-of-control Congress, requiring them to live under the same budget constraints as families and businesses.

THE TAKING BACK OUR STREETS ACT: An anti-crime package including stronger truth-in-sentencing [laws], "good faith" exclusionary rule exemptions, effective death penalty provisions, and cuts in social spending for [a recent] "crime" bill to fund prison construction and additional law enforcement to keep people secure in their neighborhoods and kids safe in their schools.

THE PERSONAL RESPONSIBILITY ACT: Discourage illegitimacy and teen pregnancy by prohibiting welfare to minor mothers and denying increased AFDC [Aid to Families with Dependent Children] for additional children while on welfare, cut spending for welfare programs, and enact a tough two-years-and-out provision with work requirements to promote individual responsibility.

THE FAMILY REINFORCEMENT ACT: Child support enforcement, tax incentives for adoption, strengthening rights of parents in their children's education, stronger child pornography laws, and an elderly dependent care tax credit to reinforce the central role of families in American society.

THE AMERICAN DREAM RESTORATION ACT: A $500-per-child tax credit, begin repeal of the marriage tax penalty, and creation of "American Dream Savings Accounts" to provide middle class tax relief.

THE NATIONAL SECURITY RESTORATION ACT: No U.S. troops under UN command and restoration of the essential parts of our national security funding to strengthen our national defense and maintain our credibility around the world.

THE SENIOR CITIZENS FAIRNESS ACT: Raise the Social Security earnings limit, which currently forces seniors out of the work force, repeal the 1993 tax hikes on Social Security benefits and provide tax incentives for private long-term care insurance to let Older Americans keep more of what they have earned over the years.

THE JOB CREATION AND WAGE ENHANCEMENT ACT: Small business incentives, capital gains cuts and indexation, neutral cost recovery, risk assessment/cost-benefit analysis, strengthening the Regulatory Flexibility Act and unfunded mandate reform to create jobs and raise worker wages.

THE COMMON SENSE LEGAL REFORM ACT: "Loser pays" laws, reasonable limits on punitive damages, and reform of product liability laws to stem the endless tide of litigation.

THE CITIZEN LEGISLATURE ACT: A first-ever vote on term limits to replace career politicians with citizen legislators.

THE CONTRACT AND THE RESULTS

It's worth noting that the Republicans didn't promise that they would pass every item in this list of legislation—a promise that would have been impossible to guarantee. What they *did* promise was to bring the bills to the floor and debate them in good faith, as well as to implement the initial set of eight reforms on the first day of their new term. Largely as a result of this contract, the congressional Republicans won stunning victories in the 1994 election, with almost 9 million more Republican voters (and 1 million fewer Democrats) turning out than in the previous off-year election. In that one race, the GOP enjoyed a swing of 10 million votes and a fifty-four-seat pickup, regaining control of Congress for the first time in forty years.

Keeping faith with their commitment—a unique accomplishment for the modern political era—the Republican majority embraced their mandate and began to work on fulfilling their contractual obligations in earnest. House Republicans formed eleven working groups that ultimately crafted bills aimed at passing into law the specific substantive provisions detailed in the Contract. Wisely, the new majority seized on the public's broad support for the most popular items in the Contract and passed them as quickly as possible, to garner momentum to complete the remainder of their task.[3] They brought all ten items to a vote in the first one hundred days of their term. Nine of the ten passed the House, the exception being the bill on term limits, which got a plurality but failed to get the two-thirds majority required for a constitutional amendment. As a testament to the unity and commitment of the Republican signatories to the Contract, once elected they managed to prevail in 299 of 302 roll call votes on issues related to the Contract.[4]

Specifically, the majority did succeed in limiting the terms for committee chairmen and the Speaker; cutting the legislative staff; reducing committee sizes; eliminating many perks; forcing Congress to live under the same laws as the rest of the nation (including OSHA, disabilities, and workplace laws); securing an audit of the U.S. House's finances by a Big Six accounting firm; balancing the budget for the first time in a generation; passing a line-item veto and signing it into law; and increasing military spending for the first time in ten years, which included funding for missile defense.[5]

Nor were these changes merely pro forma. It's a big deal for the House to have subjected themselves to laws applicable to the rest of the country. Grassroots activists pushing for this today in Congress should be advised that they're not reinventing the wheel.

It was also significant that they reduced the number of committees and their staff personnel by one-third each. The House audit was also more than just meaningless paperwork. Price Waterhouse discovered 2,200 instances of double payments for travel expenses, seven hundred pay hikes that were applied retroactively in violation of the rules, and greatly outmoded accounting practices.[6]

Never before had such a detailed document formed the

blueprint for widely divergent congressional elections through-out the nation. Never had so many relatively new ideas been incorporated into legislation with such speed, nor passed so quickly by the House.[7] *New York Times* columnist R. W. Apple, Jr., wrote, "Perhaps not since the start of the New Deal, to which many of the programs now under attack can trace their origins, has Congress moved with such speed on so many fronts."[8]

Both the idea of the Contract and its execution were noth-ing short of brilliant. And bold! After all the liberal Democratic demagoging and Republican fecklessness I'd witnessed over the years, I was truly shocked to watch as the newly invigorated Republican Party stuck to its guns even under the charge of heartlessness. One columnist, for example, described the title "Job Creation and Wage Enhancement Act" and other bills under the Contract as "warm, fuzzy names to cover the snarling face of their ripper legislation."[9] *Time* ran a cover story vilifying Newt Gingrich as "The Gingrich Who Stole Christmas," saying that "the incoming Speaker of the House [had set] off a race to cut programs for the poor. But most Americans don't agree with harsh cutbacks."

How "harsh" did they turn out to be? History is the best judge.

This Congress was determined to reform welfare, Medicare, and other entitlements, believing that to ignore them would end up bankrupting the nation. Who would have ever thought they could make headway on reforming these dependency programs—long known as the "third rail" of American politics—which are almost impossible to shrink once they're firmly in place?

But the 104th Congress didn't just end these entitlements cold turkey. Wisely, they weaned the nation off each program gradually, putting transitional measures in place to minimize the pain. The House offered a plan called Medicare Plus, which involved raising premiums for beneficiaries while encouraging the elderly to shift to private health plans. The Senate Finance Committee, following the lead of Gingrich's House, offered Medicare Choice along the same lines. Recalcitrant Democrats reached into their familiar bag of tricks and pulled out the class-warfare card, warning, in the words of Democratic congressman Sam Gibbons, that "all of these cuts will go to fund that enormous—I would say obscene—tax cut you voted out early this year."[10]

One of the major bills in the Contract was the Job Creation and Wage Enhancement Act, which was designed to reduce certain aspects of the federal government's oppressive control over the states. One of its main provisions was to put an end to unfunded mandates—the insidious laws that force states and municipalities to engage in this or that program or regulation without providing them money with which to fund them. Unfunded mandates were too seductive for congressmen to resist, knowing they could claim the credit for all kinds of ostensibly beneficial legislation in a manner that was initially fiscally painless to the federal government. The Congressional Budget Office calculated that such programs burdened states and cities between $8.9 billion and $12.7 billion from 1983 to 1990, and there was no end in sight.[11]

The Job Creation and Wage Enhancement Act also implemented amendments to tax laws and other regulations designed to bolster private property rights and boost the economy. It included, among other provisions, a 50 percent capital gains rate cut, as well as indexing capital gains to inflation, and a significant increase in investment write-offs for small business.[12]

But the centerpiece of the Contract was welfare reform. Since

LBJ's War on Poverty in 1965, the government had spent $5.5 trillion trying to eradicate poverty, but had made no dent in the problem and probably exacerbated it. The main stumbling block problem was what scholar Robert Rector, a leading national authority on poverty, called a "moral hazard," or, alternatively, "an incentive program from Hell."[13] The government's antipoverty programs tended to stimulate the very socially undesirable behaviors they rewarded, such as laziness, divorce, and illegitimacy. Thus began a vicious cycle: As each social problem grew worse, the government threw more and more money at it, like someone trying to use gasoline to extinguish a fire. We were paying the poor to continue engaging in the behavior that contributed to their poverty; the result was that they remained poor, and likely became poorer.

The Contract's solution to this problem, the Personal Responsibility and Work Opportunity Reconciliation Act of 1996, prohibited welfare to mothers under the age of eighteen, ended the increase of benefits to mothers with each additional illegitimate child, and cut welfare spending. It replaced the Aid to Families with Dependent Children welfare program (AFDC) with a block grant program called Temporary Assistance to Needy Families, allowing states to design their own systems, provided they were intended to end welfare as an entitlement and required recipients to begin working within two years of receiving benefits. The larger purpose was to end government's role in contributing to the dependency and poverty cycle. The specific goals were to reduce child poverty, teenage pregnancies, and illegitimate births. The history section of the bill stated, "In place of the entitlement concept, the new law creates two block grants that provide States with the funds necessary to help families escape welfare."[14]

How successful was the bill at reducing dependency and poverty?

Remarkably so. LBJ's War on Poverty had notoriously failed to reduce the dependency cycle. In the thirty years since it was instituted, it had increased the rolls up to five million families. One of its worst aspects was that it created intergenerational dependence: Studies clearly indicate that prolonged dependence harms the development of children, and the programs of the 1960s made welfare dependence a kind of family inheritance. One primary goal of the Contract's reform bill was to disrupt this intergenerational pattern by getting people off the rolls and back to work—and married. By that standard, the bill proved highly successful, causing welfare caseloads to decline by 56 percent by 2006, and leading to a marked increase in the employment of single mothers.

In addition, the bill made great strides in the battle against unwed childbearing. In 1965 the unwed birthrate was 7.7 percent and it grew by roughly 1 percent a year until the time of the reform bill. At that rate it would have reached 41.6 percent by 2003, but between 1995 and 2003, according to Heritage Foundation scholars Christine Kim and Robert Rector, the rate increased by only 2.4 percent total, and the black unwed childbearing rate fell 1.7 percent.[16] Kim and Rector reject the notion that these trends were a result of strong economic growth, which they say has not historically reduced welfare dependence.

The bill's other goals were met as well. The child poverty rate fell from 20.8 percent in 1995 to 17.8 percent in 2004, lifting 1.6 million children out of poverty, largely as a result of families leaving welfare and mothers beginning to work.[15] Significantly, black children and children from single-mother families experienced an unprecedented decline in poverty—contrasted with the years 1971 through 1995, where there was no such decline. For African American children the poverty rate declined from 41.5 percent to 30 percent, and for children from single-mother families from 53.1 percent to 39.8 percent—their lowest levels in our national history.

On many levels, then, the Contract was a hugely important success story. So it's regrettable, and ironic, that Republicans never managed to communicate its message to the people it helped the most: African Americans and the poor. The Contract is an object lesson in how the supposedly good intentions of liberalism pale in comparison to the "tough love" principles of conservatism. Who is more compassionate—he who professes to care, but simply diverts taxpayers' money into programs that *increase* one's dependence on government, or he who helps wean dependents off the dependency cycle, out of poverty, and back to work and self-respect?

In part, the Republicans' communication failures began in the contentious back-and-forth between Gingrich and President Bill Clinton during the government shutdowns of 1995, which were largely caused by Clinton but which many blamed unfairly on Gingrich. Clinton also shrewdly, if unconscionably, stole credit for Republican reforms that he actively opposed. When campaigning in 1992, Clinton promised to "end welfare as we know it"—a theme he proudly reiterated in his 1993 State of the Union address. "We have to end welfare as a way of life and make it a path to independence and dignity."

But Clinton waited a year and a half after the election before proposing welfare legislation, and when he did, it was hardly a reform proposal. Clinton's bill would have increased welfare spending $14 billion over five years, according to the CBO.

Adding insult to injury, especially in light of his cynical campaign promises, he vetoed Republican reform bills twice (on December 6, 1995, and January 9, 1996), before signing one into law on July 31, 1996.[17] Thereafter, he never tired of taking credit for the measure, as if he'd personally drafted the legislation himself and gallantly shoved it through Congress over fierce Republican opposition.

Nonetheless, there are lessons to be learned from Clinton through this episode. Though there's good reason to doubt Clinton's sincerity in promising to end welfare as we know it, he did show how such reforms can be successfully approached. When he was *for* reform—before he was *against* it—he used the issue as his key credential to position himself as a centrist Democrat. According to *New York Times* reporter Jason DeParle, Clinton considered welfare reform an "all-purpose elixir" for his presidential campaign, combining the messages of values, economics, and policy into one all-purpose promise. This one message reportedly resonated with the public more than any other he pushed. During the first presidential campaign, Clinton commissioned pollster Celinda Lake to conduct black voter focus groups to determine whether his pledge to end welfare could backfire on him as a racist message. On the contrary, Lake discovered that. "the welfare message, worded correctly, plays extremely well in the black community."[18]

Are you listening, Republicans?

While Clinton's sincerity on welfare reform is debatable, Robert Rector argues that his "values talk helped jump start a decline in welfare dependence." He helped create a climate for national leaders to preach that it was unwed childbearing, not race, that was the major culprit in our welfare problems.

Despite himself, then, Clinton may have provided a blueprint for future reforms. It's especially difficult for Republicans to make headway in the African American community when Democrats lie to them so shamelessly, claiming that "George Bush let people die on rooftops in New Orleans because they were poor and because they were black"(as Democrat Claire McCaskill claimed in 2006),[19] and promoting slanderous slogans like "Vote for a Republican and another black church will burn."

That said, Republicans must do a better job of approaching African Americans and other minorities—not by pandering to them or patronizing them from a race perspective, as liberal Democrats do, but relating to them on the level of values, as Bill Clinton purported to do. After all, there are large numbers of black Americans who are far more conservative than their party-line votes would indicate. And conservative solutions—not just in welfare, but also in education, health care, and across the board—are superior to liberal ones.

Here, again, we can look to Ronald Reagan for wisdom and direction. As Reagan said in 1977,

the time has come for Republicans to say to black voters: "Look, we offer principles that black Americans can, and do, support." We believe in jobs, real jobs; we believe in education that is really education; we believe in treating all Americans as individuals and not as stereotypes or voting blocs—and we believe that the long-range interest of black Americans lies in looking at what each major party has to offer, and then deciding on the merits. The Democratic Party takes the black vote for granted. Well, it's time black America and the New Republican Party move toward each other and create a situation in which no black vote can be taken for granted.[20]

Amen!

And the same can be said for other issues Bill Clinton co-opted. He also took (and still enjoys) credit for balancing the budget, which he never would have accomplished except under coercion from the Gingrich Congress. Even his projected budgets for the "out years" were astronomical for those days. In truth, Clinton never even aspired to balance the budget; Democrats rarely do. Now that Barack Obama has shown what his party does when it gains total control, this is another issue we must reclaim from Democrats.

AN ENDURING REVOLUTION?

Newt Gingrich, a historian in his own right, said of the Contract, "There is no comparable congressional document in our two-hundred year history." It's not just Gingrich himself who understands the historical significance of that 1994 pledge. My Fox News colleague Major Garrett even devoted a book to the subject: *The Enduring Revolution: How the Contract with America Continues to Shape the Nation.*

For most Americans, Garrett wrote, the Republican Revolution involved a "bright flash of power; bravado and hubris; a clash with an eloquent president; a few midcourse compromises; a massive political overreach on the budget; an inglorious retreat; and a reelected president." As Garrett makes clear, however, that's a very incomplete picture. In support, he quotes Douglas Brinkley, the University of New Orleans historian and presidential scholar: "We live in a Contract with America world. And if you look at Clinton and George W. Bush, they are successful in response to co-opting or working within a Contract with America framework of less government, lower taxes, and aggressive foreign policy. The Contract with America is the most important domestic political document of the last forty years."

That's a strong statement. Yet, as Garrett points out, "the 1994 election did indeed mark a seismic shift in American politics." Though many believe that the Republican Revolution petered out quickly after the Contract, Garrett argues that it was "the most important political story in decades . . . [but] also one of the most misunderstood episodes in our political history." Indeed, he says, "some of the most consequential moments of Republican rule of Congress occurred *after* 1995. . . . At a minimum the Republicans who took control of Congress in 1995 fundamentally changed the American debate on a host of issues—welfare, taxes, abortion, defense, health care, education, entitlements, terrorism, gun control, and crime, among others."

Even after Reagan's presidency, Garrett argues, our government still reflected FDR's New Deal principles more than Reagan's: "government is not the solution to the problem; government is the problem." It took the Republican Revolution to begin the systematic dismantling of the New Deal and LBJ's Great Society. And, despite the pace of their reforms, the Republicans were continuing to make strides more than a decade after the Contract, when Garrett published his book.

The Republicans of the 1990s and early 2000s changed policy on a wide spectrum of issues, reflecting their beliefs in the power of personal savings and personal responsibility, and in promoting individual choice in health care and retirement. In 2004, Garrett concluded, "The Contract not only lives, it governs—on both sides of the aisle. . . . Republicans have changed this country and our lives in startling ways. All of our lives, from rich, to middle-class, to poor, from conservative to liberal, from pro-life to pro-choice and pro-gun to anti-gun, from globalist to protectionist, and from hawk to dove."

Yet much has changed on this front since the 2008 election—and not for the better. In my view, those years witnessed another "seismic shift" in American politics, one that sent us careening off in a dangerous direction.

Now it's our job to get us back on the right track.

SEVEN

HOW THE REPUBLICANS LOST THEIR WAY

Few things are permanent in our political landscape, except perhaps for the constant division between the defining philosophies of liberalism and conservatism. Whatever efforts conservatives make, liberalism is not easily turned away. Whether liberal politicians are in the ascendancy or in steep decline, their foot soldiers are relentless, and patient when they need to be. Liberals can be defeated, but never permanently—absent a nationwide conversion that would make the Great Awakening look like a small-town church service. Their principles must be fought every day, and even then there's no guarantee we'll stay ahead of them. Even if we push them back several steps—even when their programs fail, or their leaders deceive or disappoint them—they will always find a way to inch back up.

LIBERALS . . . AND THE REPUBLICANS WHO IMITATE THEM

Liberals are crafty: adept at turning every failure into a triumph, at least in terms of public perception. It was liberal policies that led to our stalemate and ultimately defeat in Vietnam, but the lesson liberal professors and media taught society was that the antiwar communist sympathizers had been right from the beginning. It was liberals who said we could withdraw from Vietnam without risking significant bloodshed—John Kerry himself preached as much in his Senate testimony upon returning from Vietnam—but our departure invited a bloodbath in South Vietnam and Cambodia, where millions died. But today, despite the record, many millions more share the liberal belief that history has vindicated the liberals and their antiwar position.

The same thing has been true with entitlements—and education. For decades, liberals have been throwing money at our nation's social problems, and increasing federal control of social services. When the results are horrendous—objectively so—they demand even more money and greater federal control, and as Republicans compete to prove themselves equally "compassionate," the liberals' demands are often met. The same goes for health care: Over the years, liberals have pushed for increased government intervention, and passed "well-meaning" tax laws that have interfered with and suppressed market forces. Now that health-care costs are exploding—largely because of their tinkering with the market—they're demanding full-blown government intervention.

This is how good the liberal propaganda machine is: Even when their policies fail, somehow our society never quite repudiates liberalism.

Despite the remarkable success of the welfare reform measures of the 1990s, Barack Obama has managed to pass legislation—quietly—to reverse them. That's right: People may not realize it, but he has reversed the Contract with America's triumphant legislative measures in rolling back the dependency cycle. Obama's stimulus bills were designed to restore an AFDC-style funding system.[1] The federal government will soon start paying states bonuses to *increase* their welfare caseloads. Are you listening? Obama has restored the incentives to get people *back on* the welfare rolls. It doesn't matter a whit to him how successful welfare reform was in getting people back into the workforce and supporting themselves, reducing illegitimacy and child poverty. His unbending ideology tells him that the status quo is unacceptable unless the government is arranging for wealth to be redistributed from the "evil" wealthy to the less fortunate.

But there's also another contributing factor to the perseverance of liberalism: Republicans—at least Beltway Republicans—just cannot seem to stand political prosperity. Even when they're flying high, as they were after the 2004 elections, many Republican leaders still seem to be afraid of their own shadows. They refuse to answer the constant pounding of liberal moralizing and the pressure of political correctness. When confronted by the allegation that conservatives lack compassion, they simply fold their cards and walk away.

Even when Republicans have acted resolutely and shown confidence in their convictions, they still haven't done an effective job of responding to liberal assaults. We saw this throughout George W. Bush's entire presidency. Bush was admirably solid and unwavering in his positions on the war and taxes, to the point that it drove Democrats crazy. No matter how often they accused him of being stubborn and unwilling to admit his "mistakes," he pushed forward unflappably, even when many in his own party didn't always defend him.

But mere confidence and moral certitude weren't enough for Bush and his party to combat the Democrats' propaganda attacks. I can't tell you how frustrated we conservatives were as the left heaved volley after volley of lies against President

Bush's handling of the war, only to see the president and his party barely lift a finger in his defense. Graciousness and civility are admirable qualities, but this wasn't a game of beanbag. We weren't just fighting the war on terror; we were fighting an internal enemy—the left, which was doing everything it could to undermine our war effort and discredit President Bush for its own partisan purposes.

I fought the Democrats' propaganda fiercely on my own shows, exposing their duplicity for denouncing a war they had originally supported and for accusing President Bush of misleading about WMD when they'd seen the very same intelligence and expressed the same damning conclusions about Saddam Hussein. But no matter how faithfully I defended the Republicans, they never matched their fervor with my own. I think President Bush deserves respect for treating the office of the presidency with such dignity, and for refusing to get down in the dirt with his shameless tormentors, but at some point the Republicans should have come out strongly defending their positions.

At least Dick Cheney has been going at it with some vigor now that he and President Bush are out of office, perhaps making up for lost time. Cheney's statements defending the administration's national security policy have been strong and convincing, and the left's angry, demonizing reaction to them only further demonstrates how quickly they stoop to savage people who dare to challenge their orthodoxy. But the former vice president has remained true to his principles, despite the left's endless brutal assaults.

Still, when Bush and Cheney were in office and the leftist attacks were coming thick and fast—on Iraq, on other national security issues, and on the economy—Republicans forfeited the public relations battle. Instead of regrouping, the party leaders started falling into liberal-lite mode again. Some even echoed the Democrats' criticisms, piling on the administration, the military, and the CIA for "torture" and prisoner "abuse." They should have been shaming Democrats for making such damnable, unsupportable allegations.

Republican leaders were very ineffective in countering liberal attacks with the obvious rejoinders: that everyone, including Democrats and all the world's intelligence agencies, believed Saddam had WMD, based on the best intelligence we had, and that the administration was reasonable in acting on that intelligence. The Republican leaders never made a simple, clear declaration of their position: "The intelligence we acted on may have been flawed; we didn't know that at the time, and neither did any of our allies. But we acted prudently and in accordance with our national security interests." Instead they held their heads between their legs as if they *had* committed a fraud—as if Bush had intentionally misled Congress about WMD to justify his plan to attack Iraq. The Republicans' failure to answer the Democrats' outrageous charges contributed to the Republican Party's losing faith with the public, which in turn contributed to their defeats in 2006 and 2008.

They lost sight of one of the key principles of politics: It's not just about doing the right thing. It's about *defending your decisions,* especially when you're under relentless attack.

Likewise, Republican leaders did a terrible job of deflecting liberal populist attacks on President Bush when he tried to reform Social Security; they let stand the left's campaign to scare seniors, whom the left has since thrown under the bus with Obamacare and its inevitable rationing. And how often have you heard Republican politicians challenge the liberals' myth that we have 47 million Americans without health insurance, when we've seen data demonstrating that the actual number of those who want coverage and can't afford it is 8–12 million?

Even when Republicans did defend their positions, their defenses were often ineffective, because they allowed Democrats to define the terms and hold the debate on their turf. Before the battle was truly joined, they gave up debating whether cataclysmic, man-made global warming was occurring; anxious not to appear out of step with the "scientific consensus," they simply conceded the point and moved on to debate how best to remedy it. Nor did they bother pointing out how fantastic and extreme some of the left's claims were concerning the issue.

Don't get me wrong, the Republican leaders' refusal to defend themselves wasn't the only problem during the Bush years. There was also the fact that too many Republicans seemed to care more about being loved and considered compassionate than about good policies and good judgment. In too many areas, they were nearly as government-oriented as their rivals across the aisle. As much as I revered President Bush for his national security and tax policies, I was never enamored of his claims of "compassionate conservatism." He was not conservative enough on spending and he even began a new entitlement for prescription drugs. True, he tried to engineer Social Security reform, he cut the deficit in half before the date he had promised to do so, and the deficits would have been much larger under the Democrats (as we've now seen). But he still failed to get federal spending under control—and we conservatives were furious about it.

The Democrats' constant fraudulent assault on Bush over Iraq and the economy, coupled with the Republicans' spending practices, were a combustible combination. Compounding the problem were the rhythms of the American electoral process: With only one exception, Americans have always punished the party in power in what have become known as the "sixth-year itch" elections.[2]

So it seemed almost inevitable that the Republican Party got trounced in the 2006 congressional elections; having failed to learn their lesson, they let the same thing happen in 2008. After that second GOP defeat, the American Issues Project conducted a survey of early and likely voters in four swing states. "The Survey found that approximately 72 percent of those voters agreed that: 'The Republican Party used to stand for keeping government spending under control, but not anymore.' More than 75 percent of likely voters agreed with the statement: 'When the Republican Party took control of Congress in 1994, they promised to reform government and clean up corruption in Washington, but they failed to live up to that promise."[3] Once again, the party has failed to keep even its own best successes in the public eye.

As we've seen, the Republican Party has achieved major reforms in the past several decades. But they haven't been able to build sufficiently on those gains, nor have they been able to stop the perpetually expanding federal government—no doubt in large part due to Democrats, but also because they lost their own way. In both the 2006 and 2008 elections, Republicans were punished—"thumped," as President Bush said—for abandoning their conservative principles. Ironically, the voters turned out the Republicans for their spending excesses, only to replace them with Democrats who would dwarf them in the spending department.

The Republican Party needs to recognize these failures in order to correct them. We can cry unfairness all we want, but no matter what Democratic politicians do, Republicans cannot excuse themselves by pointing the finger at their rivals. The conservative movement needs to get its own house in order—both by cleansing the GOP of politicians who are mired in personal and professional scandals, and by stepping up and restating its case to the American people.

WHERE ELSE HAS THE REPUBLICAN PARTY GONE WRONG?

In addition to creating a new prescription drug entitlement and failing to get discretionary domestic spending under firmer control, congressional Republicans have done little to curb earmarks. The "bridge-to-nowhere" legislation, for example, which funded a $223 million bridge to an island inhabited by only fifty people, contained 6,371 earmarks alone. When this pet project of his was challenged, Alaska senator Ted Stevens issued a subtle threat: "If we start cutting funding for individual projects, your project may be next."[4]

At the behest of President George W. Bush, the Republican Party also lost its way with the sweeping education reform bill Bush proudly called "No Child Left Behind." The bill was President Bush's baby, but in spirit and in reality it was contrary to a fundamental conservative belief—that top-down federal control is to be avoided and that throwing money at problems does not solve them. As long as the liberal National Education Association controlled the public school curriculum, there would continue to be influences in the schools that emphasized anything but academic education. Politically correct, liberal indoctrination? Perhaps. Academic excellence? No.

After the 2006 "thumping," former House majority leader Dick Armey offered his own evaluation of where Republicans had gone wrong. Armey described the 1994 GOP congressional sweep as the "the culmination of years of agitation by a relatively small group of political entrepreneurs in the House. Before we could beat the Democrats and *their* 'culture of corruption,' we had to beat the old bulls of our own party. They too were driven by a parochial vision, and had grown complacent with the crumbs offered them by the majority." Armey recalled how the Republicans' "Spirit of 94" idealism degenerated, until it was eventually replaced by political bureaucrats whose sole quest became holding on to political power. Armey attributes "the aberrant behavior and scandals that ended up defining the Republican majority in 2006" to "this shift in choice criteria from policy to political power."[5]

Congressional Republicans did lose their fiscal discipline in the budgeting process, as Armey suggests. That was a crucial blow: Fiscal responsibility was the one issue Republicans had always owned and was a crucial source of support at election time. After the Republicans' spending sprees of that period, however, the party's incumbents could no longer credibly claim the mantle of fiscal restraint. On this point, Armey had a profound insight: "I've always wondered," he said, "why Republicans insist on acting like Democrats in hopes of *retaining* political power, while Democrats act like us in order to *win*."

This is the key question I keep returning to as I review the recent history of the GOP. For some reason, it seems, the Republican leaders of today lack the discipline and courage to stick to their principles once in power. As we confront the prospect of reclaiming power in the next two elections, it is more urgent than ever that, when we do, we remember to govern as conservatives. We must not allow the enticements or inertia of Washington to seduce us into betraying our principles.

Why is this so important? Because if our leaders forget why we've sent them to Washington, the voters will give them a return ticket as quickly as the next election. When Republican Party leaders forget who they are—when they lose the courage of their convictions, abandon their principles, dilute their policy positions in that quixotic quest to be more moderate or to appeal to independents—history tells us that they lose the confidence of their constituents. The public wants principled leadership, not lukewarm uncertainty and vacillation. Look at Bob Dole's milquetoast presidential campaign, or at the first President Bush's promise of a "kinder and gentler" America, complete with his broken pledge not to impose any new taxes. And how well did centrist John McCain fare against Barack Obama? McCain was the liberals' ideal Republican: a centrist, a moderate, a guy who agreed with them on campaign finance reform and torture and was always willing to attack his fellow Republicans. But even against the most radical leftist who has ever run for the office of the presidency under the banner of one of the two major political parties, the centrist, John McCain, got trounced.

We must learn these lessons, and quit falling for the message that liberals want us to believe: that the only way for us to win is to moderate our positions. *They* never moderate their positions, after all—and they never will. As Exhibit A, consider the man they've now installed in the White House: Barack Obama, with his coterie of like-minded radicals, undertaking to dismantle every institution that has made this the greatest nation in the history of the world.

SO WHERE DOES THAT LEAVE US?

Well, to my mind, it leaves us with a marvelous opportunity—to lead America back to its true direction, by returning us to our first principles, to the Constitution and the free-market ideas on which we were founded. These ideas aren't stale, even if their presentation has sometimes been lacking. Rather, they are the defining characteristics of the American experiment.

Before we can do so, we must conquer whatever insecurities may recently have handicapped us in the marketplace of ideas. We must learn again to believe in ourselves and the superiority— yes, I said it, *superiority*—of our beliefs and our policy prescriptions. That won't be easy, but it will be easier once we remember how to trust our convictions, rather than trusting our fate to the fickle winds of politics.

As conservatives, we know what we believe—but that alone is not enough. We must be more innovative in designing policies to disentangle the tentacles of government from every aspect of our society. It's fine for us to be the Party of No when the Party of Yes completely dominates both political branches. But going forward, that won't be enough. It's time for a new, positive vision, one that's tailored to meet our current challenges, but based on our timeless principles. What we need are not cutesy gimmicks, ideas that are really soft liberalism reframed as "moderate" proposals inoffensive enough to pass through Congress. Instead we need bold, ambitious ideas that will be dynamic enough to make a difference in the real world—as bold as Ronald Reagan's vision, and as practical and effective in our time as the Contract proposals were at the time of the Republican Revolution in 1994.

In the meantime, as alarming as the Obama administration's

socialist tendencies may be, we must also look at the bright side: If Obama and his party hadn't captured such firm control of our government, they might never have had the guts, or the chance, to show America who they really are and what they believe. Their real goal—to turn America into a veritable laboratory for their failed socialist ideas—may have remained cloaked for years under a "moderate" agenda of their own, until their small victories slowly coalesced into a monolithic picture.

Instead Obama and the Democrats showed their cards early. And the outrage they created can fuel our conservative resurgence.

If we conservatives don't seize this opportunity now, we may not get another chance in the near future. That is no exaggeration. Take an informal poll of your friends and you'll find an unprecedented degree of alarm among them about the direction of this country. And the alarm isn't about a sluggish economy; it's about the possible end of the nation as we know it: the eclipse of the shining city on a hill, of the beacon of liberty.

The obstacles will be formidable. The demographics have been trending against us for a while. Democrats have made progress with the growing Hispanic voter block. They have been diverting federal monies to their war chests and manipulating the census to create districts favorable to their electoral prospects. They control a corrupt Justice Department whose attorney general has racialized the poll-watching process, and who dismissed a voter intimidation case against his Black Panther friends.[6] And they are trying to pass a Universal Voter Registration Act that will stack the deck even more in their favor, extending the vote to illegal aliens and even felons.[7]

But never underestimate the resilience of the American people. Never underestimate their willingness to fight for political and economic liberty. Yes, it will be hard for the people to resist the seductive promise of cradle-to-grave security. But this nation, unlike any other, was born in liberty, and if there is anything we crave—if there is anything we depend on—it is our independence. The flame of liberty still burns hot enough in the American heart to reignite the conservative movement. Before you allow your doubts or pessimism to overwhelm you, have another look at the projections for Republicans to make huge strides in the congressional races this fall. Has a party in such firm control as today's Democratic Party ever lost faith with the American people at such an incredible pace? I don't think so.

The table is already set for us, if we'll just believe in ourselves.

If we confront the horrors and deceptions of the Obama agenda, the suicidal policies in economics and national security, head on, it will give us all the momentum we need to overturn the Democrats in the next elections. But first we must decide how to go forward and what vehicle can best take us there.

That is where we'll turn our attention next.

PART III

Moving Forward: Reclaiming the Future

EIGHT

TO BE OR NOT TO BE: A THIRD PARTY?

As we contemplate the task that lies ahead of us—which amounts, literally, to saving the nation from socialism—we should be heartened by the fact that Democrats are jumping ship as their party loses support all across the nation. As I write this, Democratic senators Byron Dorgan and Chris Dodd have just announced their retirements. Senator Ben Nelson is reportedly having misgivings about accepting Obama's quid pro quo for his support for Obamacare. Senator Blanche Lincoln is faltering in Arkansas, and Majority Leader Harry Reid is on political life support in Nevada. And, most dramatically, in January the people of Massachusetts rejected Ted Kennedy's would-be successor, Martha Coakley, and chose her Republican rival, Scott Brown, to end the decades-old Democratic hold over that state. And the hits just keep on coming: In mid-February, Indiana senator Evan Bayh added his name to the ranks of Democrats who would not seek reelection, citing partisan rancor in Congress for his decision to drop out. He said he could "best contribute to society . . . creating jobs by helping grow a business, helping guide an institution of higher learning or helping run a charitable endeavor."

What better illustration of the failed idealism of big-government liberalism than for one of the Democrats' brightest stars to abandon his political career just one year into the unfolding of the full-blown liberal experiment in this country.

And I'm not the only one's who sees a bright future ahead. In a recent appearance on *Hannity*, Newt Gingrich revealed that former Republican National Committee chairman Haley Barbour now believes the Republicans are better positioned today to regain control of Congress than they were in January 1994, the year of the last major Republican sweep. That's big news, folks.

So the table has been set for a conservative victory. What do we do next?

As I mentioned in the introduction, the first thing we must do is resist the temptation to form a new, third party to advance our conservative agenda. I'll confess that at times the idea has seemed attractive to me. When I witness the plague of Beltway-itis infecting Republican politicians in Washington; when I see our own politicians groveling before the gods of global warming; when I see them voting themselves earmarks; when I watch them confirming radicals like Attorney General Eric Holder in deference to some phantom notion of civility; when I see them forming "Gangs of 14" that enable causes they claim to reject; when I see them joining liberals to expand, to unprecedented levels, federal expenditures for and control over education; when I see them passing even more new entitlement programs when the ones we have are already pushing us toward insolvency; when too many of them are caught in personal scandals—I sometimes wish we could throw all the bums out.

But I also realize the historical perils that path represents. It's a historical fact that the mentality driving third-party campaigns is often a negative energy, not a constructive one. It's perfectly healthy to feel deep frustration with the political class, and to want to channel that frustration into meaningful action. But often that frustration is all that unites those breakaway movements. They're content to define themselves *against* something, but when it comes time to rally around a positive vision, they find themselves unable to agree on a direction, or mired in foolishness or incoherence.

I've got a lot of respect for Ross Perot; his criticisms of government waste and complexity were admirable and timely. But his proposed solutions were often absurd and embarrassing. He professed to lead a movement based on bottom-up democracy, replete with feedback directly from the people to the White House through some technological device that would turn our system into some sort of ongoing plebiscite. What he was advocating was the closest thing to pure democracy we've seen in modern times—perhaps in all of American history—and, as you might expect, it had great populist appeal. But ultimately his ideas would have amounted to a dismantling of the United States Constitution; in a sense they were as un-American as the deficit spending and waste he was railing against.

Our framers understood that experiments in pure democracy were outright folly, a potential recipe for tyranny—as we saw in the French Revolution, which traced the slippery slope between a power-to-the-people movement and the kind of mob rule that ultimately leads back to tyranny and the guillotine. That's why our framers crafted a constitution of limited, representative government with checks and balances. It wasn't easy for them to get their unique structure of government ratified by the people, but the results have proven reliable for more than two hundred years.

The fact is that well-meaning advocates like Ross Perot sometimes let their passions and frustrations get the best of them. And that points up another Achilles' heel for third-party movements: that the personalities of their leaders can often derail their own best-laid plans. As a quintessentially top-down control guy himself, for instance, Perot was uniquely ill-suited to lead a purely democratic reform movement. He wasn't the kind of leader who would easily settle for carrying out orders dictated to him by the American people. It was obvious during the campaign that Perot didn't brook criticism or dissent too well. It's rare to find a self-described "democrat" who does.

My purpose isn't to bash Ross Perot, who is a great American. It's to illustrate that third-party movements can be very different from what they appear—and that difference sometimes doesn't come to light until the election is over and it's too late. The Perot movement was propelled by outrage over government waste and complexity, but if it had attained power and begun trying to implement its ideas, the result would have been utter chaos.

But the greatest danger of a third-party movement isn't necessarily what happens if they attain office. It's what can happen if they gain enough momentum to siphon away votes from the party they're more closely aligned with. After all, what was the most lasting contribution the Perot movement made to American politics? No, it wasn't his stance on NAFTA, or his interest in updating the Constitution, or even his idea of the "electronic town hall." No, it was that he inadvertently delivered the White House to Bill Clinton.

Today the Tea Party movement and other like-minded protests have emerged throughout the land, to answer and combat the imminent destruction of our nation by Obama and his band of radicals. I couldn't be more impressed with this grassroots development and the energy fueling it. It is truly a grassroots movement, not the artificially contrived, conspiratorial "Astroturf movement" the administration has painted. The only thing artificial anywhere near the Tea Party protests were the counterprotests Obama staged, sending in his SEIU thugs to shout down, bully, intimidate, and physically attack the Tea Party patriots.

(For the record, the idea that Obama was propelled to power through spontaneous grassroots support collapsed after the election, when the claim that he garnered millions of individual, "bottom-up" campaign contributions via the Internet was revealed as pure orchestrated hokum. As political blogger Micah Sifry has explained, "the truth is that Obama was never nearly as free of dependence on big money donors as the reporting suggested, nor was his movement as bottom-up or people-centric as his marketing implied. . . . The people who voted for him weren't organized in any kind of new or powerful way." The special interests, said Sifry, "sat first at the table and wrote the menu. Myth met reality, and came up wanting."[1])

Our Tea Party movement, on the other hand, *is* an authentic grassroots phenomenon. I agree with nearly every criticism of government the Tea Party patriots have leveled, and want to encourage them to continue their great work. But the truth is that it will take more than individual protests to seize power back from the left in the elections of 2010 and 2012. We need a coordinated, cohesive message and a smart action plan that can carry us forward. The lion's share of the ideas coming out of the Tea Party protests are indeed positive, but they lack any kind of organizational unity—which is inevitable in such a decentralized, grassroots movement. We also see, within the movement, a good amount of single-issue advocacy—the kind of passionate activism that can have the power to ignite a movement, but cannot on its own sustain a new "revolution" unless it's consolidated into a unified vision.

The Tea Party protests will continue, as I believe they should. They have been an indispensable catalyst to energize our troops to fight back. They have done more than that as well, supporting, for example, constitutionally conservative candidates against RINOs—Republicans in name only—such as helping to oust Florida's Republican Party chairman. "We are turning our guns on anyone who doesn't support constitutionally conservative candidates," said Dale Robertson, who helped start the Tea Party movement two years ago.[2]

But the conservative movement is ready for the next step—ready to coordinate these protests into a unified campaign. We need to channel the energy and spirit of the entire range of conservatives, from single-issue enthusiasts to "wide-spectrum" ones, into an integrated movement in which all will be comfortable and compatible—one that is true to genuine conservatism and doesn't gratuitously alienate any of its constituent components.

And there are messages that unite us all—chief among them the widespread outrage surrounding the explosion in the size and scope of government, and the national debt, under the Obama administration. Whatever some cynics might say, the truth is that Americans just don't want socialism. And the clearer it has become that Obama's agenda is unabashedly socialist, the more unpopular he has grown.

Obama knows this, too. That's why he's been trying to push his agenda through so urgently—because the longer it takes, the wiser people become to his schemes. He campaigned as a man of the people, one who would make the government completely transparent and a reflection of the popular will. But now that people have caught on to him and his deceitful agenda, he's had to close off the public's access to the ordinary workings of government. Congress passes bills at midnight going into weekends and vacations. Obama refuses to post the text of proposed bills on the Internet well in advance of their consideration by Congress, as he promised he would. He has proven himself a top-down autocrat with an unyielding agenda that he is determined to cram down our throats, even if it means the ouster of his party from Congress in 2010. As long as he can sign his major bills into law, and ensure their provisions begin to take effect, he clearly figures it will be too late for even a strong Republican majority to undo the radical changes he intends to make to every aspect of our society.

But as we conservatives map out our strategy to counter Obama's master plan for the irreversible conversion of this nation to socialism, we must also recognize that the battle goes far beyond economic issues. We must oppose Obama on every front, because he is chipping away at every corner of our American constitutional system, and every aspect of our liberties. In response we need every hand we can muster to counter his efforts and rebuild our system with our own positive action plan.

Obama and his party stand for America's economic bankruptcy, virtual surrender in the war on terror, and a culture of death, from abortion to embryonic stem cell research to health-care rationing tantamount to death panels. He stands for a comprehensive radicalization of our culture, from turning our schools over to homosexual activists, to undermining the sanctity of heterosexual marriage, to expanding the dependency classes. He stands for polarization and alienation between racial and ethnic groups, and between those of different economic circumstances. He stands for government swallowing the private sector and equalizing income and asset distribution; he may even use the courts, if he can pull it off, to impose what he and his fellow radicals call "economic justice," a grand-scale version of "spreading the wealth around." He stands for ceding our national sovereignty to international bodies and transferring our wealth to "undeveloped" nations. He stands for largely abandoning our steadfast ally, Israel, and promoting third-world thug dictators around the world, from Hugo Chavez to Daniel Ortega to Manuel Zelaya to the Castro brothers. He stands for the government acquiring control over all aspects of our society through socialized medicine, cap-and-trade legislation, and other punitive environmental regulations.

In other words, Obama stands for a classic socialist agenda. And he has undertaken a mission that will negatively affect all aspects of our society. The one campaign promise he *does* intend to keep is to bring about fundamental change—to the point where, if his efforts aren't stopped, we will no longer be able to recognize this country.

But we cannot stop him if we allow ourselves to be divided, splintered, and dispirited through needless internal debate—the kind that would only play into Obama's hands and allow him to divide and conquer our movement. We need a broad, mainstream conservative vision that everyone on the right can embrace, from purist Libertarians to the strongest type of neoconservative. There is room within the conservative movement for many gradations of opinion, from libertarians and so-called paleoconservatives to neocons: there is much more that unites us than divides us.

Some have expressed concern that trying to define a mainstream conservative platform could turn off some committed conservatives. But I'm not worried about this, any more than Ronald Reagan was in his time. If we rally around the principles that Reagan articulated and adapt them to the new (and old) problems of our time, I'm confident we'll be able to forge an enormous, cohesive tent that will fit us all quite comfortably while leaving room for independents and other constituencies— African Americans, Hispanics, and others—to join us.

On that note, I'm encouraged by the latest Gallup polls, which show that once again more Americans—indeed, twice as many—identify themselves as conservatives than call themselves liberals. Even more interesting, conservatives are attracting moderates to their ranks, which is something liberals said couldn't be done.[3] But it *is* being done, just as it's been done many times before. And this movement can grow, even more powerfully, if we pursue a bold, unapologetically conservative vision, one that's designed to recapture this nation from Obama and his radicals.

It's the only thing that can save the United States.

The history of the last fifty years has been one of liberals imposing a series of socialistic schemes, and of conservatives rolling them back. Every time these government encroachments have been reversed, enormous benefits have accrued to the American people. Even Ronald Reagan's tax cuts were, in a sense, a rolling back of confiscatory tax rates imposed by liberals over the years— as were John F. Kennedy's cuts two decades before. If liberals would stop tinkering with our free enterprise system and allow our constitutional system to function as the framers designed it to function, there would be far less need for us conservatives to take these dramatic, restorative steps. But we recognize our role as a watchdog for small-government discipline, and we realize that, without our efforts, the United States might long since have plunged irretrievably into socialism.

In this historical moment, there is no more important task than saving it again.

The American people have been jolted into realizing that our precious freedom is not guaranteed. There will always be forces committed to taking it away. Today we face a new array of such forces, both externally and internally. I contend that the internal threat of liberalism may be even worse than the external threat of terrorism—for the terrorists have no prayer against us unless the liberals pave their way.

In the coming election, we must allow our shared love of liberty to unite us in taking our country back.

We must make every effort to recognize, understand, and combat the threat of socialism we're facing today. We must fight the tendency to dismiss the idea that "socialism" is simply a buzzword, an antiquated idea dredged up from history to alarm patriotic Americans. Yes, through the years socialism has gone by many names: Ronald Reagan often called it "collectivism." My buddy Mark Levin calls it "statism." Others call it Marxism. Each term carries different connotations, but they all involve the core belief that government is the solution to, not the cause of, most of our problems. We cannot be accused of exaggeration when we describe our opponents as socialists, for that is what they are. By now, more than a year into the Obama administration, the American people understand that. And it is a recipe for disaster. Socialism has never worked—not here, not in the Soviet Union or China, not even in Europe. By definition, socialism cannot coexist with political liberty. And liberty is our defining value as a nation; we will choose it every time.

In the coming elections, we must hold the Obama machine accountable for fraudulently campaigning as a centrist, even as a conservative. As I've noted, it's nothing new for Democrats to masquerade as conservatives during political campaigns: Reagan pointed out how tempting it is for Democrats to run as conservatives. In 1974, as he pointed out, "Bureaucracy was assailed and fiscal responsibility hailed [throughout Democratic campaigns]. . . . But let's not be so naïve as to think we are witnessing a mass conversion to the principles of conservatism. Once sworn into office, the victors reverted to type. In their view, the ends justified the means."

Sound familiar? You bet. But Obama's efforts to market himself as a conservative couldn't erase his radical past and radical associations, or his reputation as the most liberal senator in the nation. And his radicalism could always be counted on to leak out around the edges—from his promises to "spread the wealth around" to his belief in negotiating with tyrants without preconditions to his condescension toward "bitter [Americans who] cling to guns or religion or antipathy to people who aren't like them or anti-immigrant sentiment or anti-trade sentiment as a way to explain their frustrations."[4] His liberalism was apparent to anyone who was observant and resistant to his now-legendary "cool" and conciliatory temperament.

Today, Barack Obama's true nature is apparent. And we must protect ourselves from allowing it to transform our nation into a permanent socialist state.

On the day after the 2008 election, I read on the radio an excerpt from Ronald Reagan's 1975 CPAC speech—one that bears directly on the questions we face today. In the speech, Reagan identified the timeless struggle between two competing worldviews—the struggle that still defines the political debate today. "The problem underlying all the others is the worldwide contest for the hearts and minds of mankind," he observed. "Do we find the answers to human misery in freedom as it is known, or do we sink into the deadly dullness of the Socialist ant heap?"

In the latter part of Reagan's speech, he addressed the very same challenge we face in the next two elections: how to remake and revitalize the Republican Party as the best vehicle to advance the conservative cause. As Reagan recognized, this meant a reassessment of the principles that should inform the party. At the time of his speech, the GOP was divided between the country club Republicans who were urging the party toward a moderate, big-tent approach, and Reagan and his followers, who were firm in rejecting that approach.

"I don't know about you," Reagan told his audience, "but I am impatient with those Republicans who after the last election rushed into print saying, 'We must broaden the base of our party.'" Why? Because he perceived that "broadening the base" inevitably meant "blur[ring] . . . the differences between ourselves and our opponents."

Whether it's the country club Republicans of Reagan's time, or the contemporary Republican dissenters represented by David Frum, the same is true today. When all is said and done, the path these dissenters advocate would ultimately *dilute* the appeal of conservatism, not broaden it. The more gyrations such RINOs undergo to tweak the party's platform in the name of inclusion, the more they risk transforming the GOP into a party of uncommitted, uncompelling faux Democrats.

As Reagan noted in his speech, many Republican voters had stayed home instead of voting in 1974—because they felt there wasn't a sufficient difference between the parties. I can't tell you how many callers to my show have expressed that same frustration and, as a result, refused to vote in 2006 and again in 2008.

And yet, despite these frustrations, Reagan affirmed clearly that the Republican Party was still the best vehicle to advance the conservative cause. It simply had to be revitalized, "raising a banner of no pale pastels, but bold colors which make it unmistakably clear where we stand on all the issues troubling the people." Reagan recognized that "a political party cannot be all things to all people. It must represent certain fundamental beliefs which must not be compromised to political expediency, or simply to swell its numbers." This was a highly counterintuitive message at the time, one that was less popular with establishment Republicans than with the people themselves, who look to their leaders for bold vision, not compromises designed to gain votes. Conservatism is still the dominant ideology in this nation, because it reflects most closely the great principles on which America was founded. And when it is presented as such, by leaders with the courage to stand up for their convictions instead of pandering to the cultural elite, it will prevail in every election, whether local or national.

Bold colors, not pale pastels: That's the spirit of conservatism, and it's still the formula for victory today. But what are the defining principles that constitute our bold colors in the twenty-first century? They're uncannily similar to the ones Reagan advocated in his time.

Let's take a closer look.

NINE

WHAT ARE OUR FIRST PRINCIPLES?

Some in the Republican establishment have questioned the wisdom of those of us who consider ourselves Reagan conservatives. We are stuck in the past, they say, clinging to nostalgia for a bygone period; it's time, they say, to move on to a new set of ideas and strategies for the future. Well, I'm all for reformulating our strategies and adopting new programs to deal with our current set of issues. But I reject the idea that adapting to today means throwing out the founding principles that have defined our country for more than two centuries. The three sets of overlapping conservative principles that Ronald Reagan identified in the 1970s—the three legs of the stool—are every bit as essential now as they were in Reagan's time. And they offer an instructive model for anyone trying to refine solutions to today's problems.

ECONOMIC ISSUES

In his CPAC speech, Reagan said, "Let us show that we stand for fiscal integrity and sound money and above all for an end to deficit spending, with ultimate retirement of the national debt. Let us also include a permanent limit on the percentage of the people's earnings government can take without their consent. Let our banner proclaim a genuine tax reform that will begin by simplifying the income tax so that workers can compute their obligation without having to employ legal help."

For the David Frums and David Brookses of the world, Reagan's words offer a challenge that is impossible to counter. Of course we must stand for fiscal integrity, and for sound money— and for an end to deficit spending, now more than ever. And we must *reduce,* not increase, the rate at which the government taxes our earnings. But in order to pull this off, we will have to take our case to the people—and we will have to attack, head-on, the class warfare that for years Democrats have been using to undermine the proven historical track record of conservative economic policies. Obama's outrageously reckless spending practices have made restoring fiscal integrity an urgent short-term goal, but we must craft specific strategies to accomplish a balanced budget in the near term and into perpetuity. And we cannot do that without tackling entitlements—third rail or not.

There can be no more hedging, no more mincing words. We must have a comprehensive approach to reform our unsustainable entitlement programs while reining in our discretionary spending to cover only things that are within the rightful scope of government.

Reagan continued: "Let our banner proclaim our belief in a free market as the greatest provider for the people. Let us also call for an end to the nit-picking, the harassment and over-regulation of business and industry which restricts expansion and our ability to compete in world markets. Let us explore ways to ward off socialism, not by increasing government's coercive power, but by increasing participation by the people in the ownership of our industrial machine."

Today—more than during the Cold War, more than at any other time in modern history—average Americans have begun to appreciate their political and economic freedoms, because for the first time they feel perilously close to losing them. As we study the horrific track record of socialized medicine in other countries, and examine the details of the health-care bills Obama and his Democrats are advancing, we are reminded just how precious our liberties are. We know that, despite the Obama crew's rants against the "unfair distribution of resources," the free market provides the most prosperity to the most people. It always has, and it always will.

Our free-market system is the reason that American prosperity has outshined that of every other free nation in history. And if we should abandon our faith in market forces, in favor of a command-control economy, we will forfeit that prosperity. This is a lesson we learned very early in our history, when the pilgrims discovered that people would quit working instead of being forced to share the fruits of their labor with "other men's wives and children without any recompense." [1] People don't produce when the government confiscates too great a portion of their earnings. Liberals think they can tax people without limiting the overall productivity pie, but this is yet another instance in which world history refutes their delusions. Americans instinctively recoil at the idea of government control of the private sector; that explains their reaction to Obama's power grabs over General Motors, executive salaries, and his health-care and cap-and-trade schemes. The time is ripe for conservatives to make their case— not just a rejection of Obama socialism, but a reinvigoration of free-market capitalism.

While we're at it, nothing could be more important in our effort to sell our message than to answer, once and for all, the liberal attacks on capitalism and the free market on moral grounds—including Christian grounds. Liberals, who claim to love capitalism—the same way they love the military—moralize constantly about its shortcomings, claiming that conservatives don't care about the poor, and romanticizing socialistic systems as more equitable and humane. Liberals have never been able to stomach the fact that, under a free system, some people do better than others.

In 1979, liberal television host Phil Donahue challenged the brilliant free-market economist Milton Friedman about the "greed" inherent in capitalism. In response, Friedman offered a concise seminar in the delusions of liberal thinking.

Donahue began with a leading question: "When you see around the globe the mal-distribution of wealth, the desperate plight of millions of people in underdeveloped countries, when you see so few haves and so many have-nots, when you see the greed and the concentration of power, did you ever have a moment of doubt about capitalism and whether greed's a good idea to run on?"

Friedman took Donahue to school, exposing the flaws in Donahue's entire premise. "Tell me, is there some society you know that doesn't run on greed?" the economist asked.

Do you think Russia doesn't run on greed? You think China doesn't run on greed? What is greed? Of course none of us are greedy; it's only the other fellow who's greedy. The world runs on individuals pursuing their separate interests. The great achievements of civilization have not come from government bureaus. Einstein didn't construct his theory under order from a bureaucrat. Henry Ford didn't revolutionize the automobile industry that way. In the only cases in which the masses have escaped from the kind of grinding poverty you're talking about, the only cases in recorded history are where they have had capitalism and largely free trade. If you want to know where the masses are worst off, it's exactly in the kinds of societies that depart from that. So the record of history is absolutely crystal clear: that there is no alternative way so far discovered of improving the lot of the ordinary people that can hold a candle to the productive activities that are unleashed by a free enterprise system.[2]

Donahue came at the question again, asking Friedman whether capitalism doesn't seem to reward manipulation of the system, rather than rewarding virtue. "What does reward virtue?" Friedman answered. "You think the communist commissar rewards virtue? You think a Hitler rewards virtue? . . . Is it really true that political self-interest is nobler somehow than economic self-interest? . . . Just tell me where in the world you find these angels who are going to organize society for us. I don't even trust you to do that!"[3]

No matter how much liberals wish it were otherwise, no matter how much it offends their sensibilities, no matter how many lectures they deliver on greed, the fact remains that free enterprise is the best system for producing wealth and lifting people out of poverty. The historical record is equally clear on the failure of liberal, big-government welfare programs, which are sold under the banner of compassion but ultimately do more damage than good. Through the Great Society and beyond, liberals have thrown trillions of dollars at poverty without making a dent in it. But they did go a long way toward destroying the family unit, especially in the minority community. Throwing money at people, after all, can shatter their spirit and dignity, and in the long run it rarely helps to solve their problems. This is not to say that conservatives don't believe in a social safety net, but we don't believe in reordering an entire economy based on wealth redistribution and equalization of incomes.

Another classic case of misguided liberal thinking is when they promise to help the "working poor" by increasing the minimum wage. All puffed up with righteousness, they routinely pass new laws to up the minimum—even though it's been shown that such increases invariably put people out of business and increase unemployment. By the same token, liberals regularly insist on compelling the public and private sector to provide "affordable housing" for everyone—despite the risk of wrecking an entire economy in the process. And the meltdown of the American economy has only fueled their efforts to interfere with the mortgage market—using their morally superior intentions to lead millions more borrowers into default and poverty. The sad truth is that the liberals' so-called good intentions don't produce good results. There is nothing generous about using government to take money from certain people—hardworking taxpayers—and to redistribute it to a class of government dependents.

And, without getting into a theological sermon myself, I do want to address another popular angle of attack on our capitalistic system these days: that of the new so-called "religious left." These self-righteous liberals tell us that Jesus had a heart for the poor, which is undeniable. But Jesus never directed that government be the agency used to help the poor. He was talking about charity proceeding from individuals and His church. Our liberal Christian friends would do well to remember the scriptural commandments against stealing and coveting. They might also acknowledge what countless studies have shown: that Christians and conservatives are much more charitable with their own funds than other people. I might add that liberals have little credibility in criticizing the compassion of conservatives when you consider that Obama's policies are guaranteed to bankrupt our nation and leave our children and grandchildren in poverty and slavery.

We must turn the tables on these finger-wagging liberals, who—in the interest of inflating their own egos and cravings for power—are destroying the wealth of this nation and ruining the futures of our children.

NATIONAL SECURITY

Getting back to first principles as conservatives also means re-investing in the Reagan model of peace through strength. This model, as noted, is based on a worldview that recognizes evil in the world and believes that evil regimes must be opposed, not appeased. The enemy we faced yesterday—global communism—was no more menacing than the one we face today in Islamic extremism. Just as liberals in Reagan's time (and before) dismissed the idea of a global communist conspiracy and even romanticized communist systems, liberals today recklessly downplay the nature and magnitude of the terrorist threat. On my radio show, former New York mayor Rudy Giuliani told me and my audience that he was troubled by Obama's refusal to identify the enemy as broader than Al Qaeda, which Rudy says is only one component of the Islamic extremist enemy we face. "He has yet to use the term 'Islamic extremism,' " Rudy pointed out, which brings into serious question his competence and fitness as a leader.

Obama and his fellow Democrats don't view the world in the same terms we do. They suggest that there's a moral equivalence between a few isolated cases of unauthorized enemy prisoner abuse on our side and the terrorists who beheaded innocent people for sport on their side. It is truly incomprehensible that the Democrats could regard us in any sense in the same moral category as jihadist terrorists.

Since Obama took office, he has reversed many of President Bush's prudent and effective policies in the war on terror. The consequences of such naïveté are already unfolding, as terrorist attacks on our own soil increase. When our commander in chief doesn't recognize we're at war, how can he possibly do his job of safeguarding the national security of the United States? As the editorial page editors for *Investor's Business Daily* put it, "We need a government that will fight for us."[4]

We also need a government that will quit playing footsie with foreign dictators, such as those of Iran, North Korea, and Venezuela. We need a government that is recognized by all as being true to its word, as opposed to issuing empty threats and imposing insincere deadlines.

But it will be difficult for the current administration to change direction in these areas. The White House appears mired in its blame-America-first mentality; in Obama's view, America is the one with unjustified nuclear blood on its hands and has no more moral right to "the bomb" than any other brutish dictatorship in the world.

Conservatives, on the other hand, recognize that we live in a dangerous world, and that the world will always be dangerous because human beings are fallen. The nuclear genie is out of the bottle; the world has changed; much as we would like, we can never return to a world without nuclear weapons. Our primary enemy employs asymmetrical warfare, with soldiers sprinkled around the globe, always looking for opportunities to acquire weapons of mass destruction. Loving death as much as we love life, they are completely immune from any deterrents—even nuclear deterrents—we might attempt to use to dissuade them from the suicide missions they consider part of their holy duty.

SOCIAL POLICY

Conservatives, being God-fearing at their core, are committed to protect the sanctity of innocent human life. I do not share the belief that we should "turn down the volume" when it comes to defending the unborn. We support the concept of traditional marriage, between one man and one woman, as one of the essential institutions of a stable, ordered society. We also believe, above all, in the traditional family as the foundational unit in our society. We must not allow government to continue to undermine the nuclear family, as it has with welfare programs that provide incentives for people to remain unmarried, quit working, and produce illegitimate children. These are horrible results in the name of compassion. You don't help people by destroying their dignity and their family. As Reagan said,

> Families—not government programs—are the best way to make sure our children are properly nurtured, our elderly are cared for, our cultural and spiritual heritages are perpetuated, our laws are observed and our values are preserved. . . . [The] government's programs, actions, officials and social welfare institutions [must] never be allowed to jeopardize the family. We fear the government may be powerful enough to destroy our families; we know that it is not powerful enough to replace them. The New Republican Party must be committed to working always in the interest of the American family.[5]

THE CONSTITUTION

Finally, mainstream conservatives also believe in our unique constitution—the document that British prime minister William Gladstone described as "the most wonderful work ever struck off at a given time by the brain and purpose of man."[6] Conservatives consider our founding document an expression of the framers' clear understanding of man's fallen nature. As Alexander Hamilton wrote in *Federalist* 51, "If men were angels, no government would be necessary. If angels were to govern men, neither external nor internal controls on government would be necessary. In framing a government which is to be administered by men over men, the great difficulty lies in this: you must first enable the government to control the governed; and in the next place oblige it to control itself."[7]

As a result, the framers crafted a form of government that would pit coequal branches of government against one another in competing roles, in order to prevent any branch from acquiring too much power at the expense of the others. That was the best way to establish and preserve individual liberty while at the same time investing the government with sufficient powers to carry out its necessary functions. Conservatives believe that the maintenance of the structural integrity of the Constitution is essential to preserving the separation of powers and our system of federalism, which, in turn, are essential to preserving our liberties.

It is for this reason that conservatives favor originalist judges, those who interpret the Constitution according to the original meaning of the document—not as stubborn legalist purists, but as students of government and history who understand that such a document cannot retain its authority unless its actual text is honored. When the meanings of a constitutional passage are softened or blurred, abuses will follow and erosions of power will occur—powers that are essential to maintaining the proper balances among the branches and levels of government. When activist judges make up the law as they go—when they legislate instead of interpreting the law—they compromise the structural integrity of the Constitution and undermine the balance that was designed to ensure our liberties. Nothing is more important to our conservative philosophy than reverence for the Constitution as the indispensable bulwark of our liberties.

THE REAL IDEOLOGUES AND EXTREMISTS

Our beliefs as conservatives, then, are clear and firm. Does that make us extremists?

This is a charge that has been leveled at the modern conservative movement from its very beginnings—that true conservatives dwell only on the fringes of society, that their beliefs are unrealistic at best and dangerous at worst. The liberals in Washington, and in the mainstream media, have been pushing this line at least since the days of Barry Goldwater. And we must be prepared to answer it—to demonstrate that our principles, far from being extreme, are fundamentally American.

Were our framers extreme? Perhaps so, if only because they were founding a new nation in a world dominated by monarchies, oligarchies, tyrannies, and oppression. They were carving out a new space for freedom in a world where liberty was radical in theory and scarce in practice.

But that was nearly two hundred and fifty years ago. The civilized world has long since caught up with our framers' unbending commitment to freedom; liberty is no longer an extreme political demand, but rather the fundamental human right. And we mainstream conservatives merely carry the same torch our forefathers did. We believe in adhering to the Constitution as written; in maximizing our liberties within the context of law; in maintaining a strong defense; and in traditional values and a strong, unwavering faith in God. We endorse policies that are proven to have worked to maximize liberty, foster economic growth, strengthen our national defense, and preserve our orderly, morally healthy, and stable society.

Ronald Reagan argued that we must challenge the media's depiction of conservatives as extremists, lest such negative perceptions discredit us and undermine our cause. "If we allow ourselves to be portrayed as ideological shock troops without correcting this error," he said, "we are doing ourselves and our cause a disservice. Wherever and whenever we can, we should gently but firmly correct our political and media friends who have been perpetuating the myth of conservatism as a narrow ideology." [8]

And, in my view, if we express these principles clearly and firmly, another reward will follow: Moderate and centrist Americans will feel genuinely comfortable among us. For the truth is that our beliefs are straightforward, grounded in moral clarity and common sense, and worthy of a wide and deep following. Indeed, our task is not so much to convert people to our cause, but to make them realize—by clearly articulating our principles and countering the propaganda that exists about us—that they already share most of our beliefs.

A true conservative should not be exclusionary. It's one thing to stick to our principles; it's another to exclude others from supporting the causes we share, just because they don't agree with us on every issue. We don't have to alter our core beliefs in order to open our arms graciously to those who share our fundamental vision. Reagan understood the importance of "our friends who are now Republicans but who do not identify themselves as conservatives," and sought to reassure them that "the new revitalized Republican Party [would not be] based on a principle of exclusion. . . . Conservatism is not a narrow ideology, nor is it the exclusive property of conservative activists."[9]

No, the true blind ideologues in today's society are liberals, who continue to push for policies and programs long after decades of painful experience have proven that they don't work. As Reagan said, "Ideology . . . always conjures up in my mind a picture of a rigid, irrational clinging to abstract theory in the face of reality. We have to recognize that in this country 'ideology' is a scare word. And for good reason. Marxist-Leninism is, to give but one example, an ideology. . . . If the facts don't happen to fit the ideology, the facts are chopped off and discarded."[10]

But his next sentence was perhaps his most important:

I consider [blind ideology] to be the complete opposite to principled conservatism. If there is any political viewpoint in this world which is free from slavish adherence to abstraction, it is American conservatism. When a conservative states that the free market is the best mechanism ever devised by the mind of man to meet material needs, he is merely stating what a careful examination of the real world has told him is the truth. When a conservative says that totalitarian Communism is an absolute enemy of human freedom he is not theorizing—he is reporting the ugly reality captured so unforgettably in the writings of Alexander Solzhenitsyn. When a conservative says it is bad for the government to spend more than it takes in, he is simply showing the same common sense that tells him to come in out of the rain. When a conservative says that busing does not work, he is not appealing to some theory of education—he is merely reporting what he has seen down at the local school. When a conservative quotes Jefferson that government that is closest to the people is best, it is because he knows that Jefferson risked his life, his fortune and his sacred honor to make certain that what he and his fellow patriots learned from experience was not crushed by an ideology of empire.

Amen.

And a similar litany can be offered today:

When a conservative rejects the Keynesian folly of "priming the pump" through deficit spending, he does so based on common sense and experience. History has demonstrated not only that deficit spending doesn't work, but that it's actively destructive—not to mention the fact that it runs against basic reasoning. In government as in our private lives, we have no business spending more than we take in.

When a conservative advocates peace through strength and rejects appeasement, he does so based on a worldview that recognizes the existence of good and evil in the world, and on our shared historical experience that the appeasement of tyrants is both immoral and dangerous. It is no less an application of common sense to stand up to bullies on the international stage than it is in the schoolyard. The moment your adversaries lose respect for you is the moment your liberty will be compromised.

When a conservative says that reducing income tax rates can increase the overall revenue pie, he is basing his statement not on wishful thinking, but on countless examples in our history of the success of such supply-side policies. When a liberal opposes such policies, it's not because they don't work, but because they interfere with his rigid ideology—his belief that government should take the leading role in distributing wealth.

When a conservative promotes cutting or eliminating capital gains taxes, he does so not just because such taxes are another form of double taxation and inconsistent with our rights to private property, but because cutting capital gains has proven to increase revenues. When Obama and other liberals oppose capital gains rate cuts, they do so—by their own admission—because they value other things above economic growth, revenue, and overall prosperity. They base their decision on their value judgment that it's better that everyone suffer equally, rather than some benefit more than others—a classic Marxist position, as painful as that is to say.

When a conservative advocates rolling back welfare, it's because he has learned from history that increasing an individual's dependence on government is unhealthy for both individuals and society and is terribly destructive to the family unit. But does that matter to liberals? No, because their ideology tells them that government must be the caretaker of the people, as they are incapable of taking care of themselves.

When conservatives call for market solutions for health care and rejects the socialized-medicine model, we do so after comparing the American experience with that of every society that has tried socialized medicine—to disastrous effect. We understand that, in addition to destroying the quality and quantity of health care, such measures always result in a radical reduction of personal freedom. When liberals persist in pushing socialized medicine, they fly in the face of the historical record. And they justify their decision only by lying, either to themselves or to society.

When a conservative disputes the absolutism of the global warming fanatics, he does so based on both legitimate science and common sense. Republicans who have rushed to jump on the global warming bandwagon for the sake of ingratiating themselves to the liberal elite have only undermined the pursuit of truth and enabled the adoption of economically devastating and senseless policies based on very disputed science. When liberals declare the existence of a false scientific consensus on global warming, they are perpetrating an enormous fraud: It is they themselves, not the skeptics, who are the real flat-earthers in the debate. When they support policies that will destroy our economy, transfer wealth to third-world nations without even helping those nations ultimately to help themselves, and suggest that we wastefully and foolishly forgo our own available energy resources, they are advocating a devastating course for America— all for no appreciable difference in the global environment.

How can people embrace such insanity?

The truth is clear: It is the American liberal, not the American conservative, who is actually trapped by ideology. This is why, instead of debating the facts, liberals retreat to their emotions and respond with their empty, moralizing lectures.

We conservatives must remember the simple fact that we are merely peddlers of common sense, advocates of policy that's based on the wisdom of experience. We are anything but extreme.

As Ronald Reagan put it,

The common sense and common decency of ordinary men and women, working out their own lives in their own way— this is the heart of American conservatism today. Conservative wisdom and principles are derived from the willingness to learn, not just from what is going on now, but from what has happened before. The principles of conservatism are sound because they are based on what men and women have discovered through experience in not just one generation or a dozen, but in all the combined experience of mankind.

"When we conservatives say that we know something about political affairs, and that we know can be stated as principles, we are saying that the principles we hold dear are those that have been found, through experience, to be ultimately beneficial for individuals, for families, for communities and for nations—found through the often bitter testing of pain, or sacrifice and sorrow.[11]

How true—and how relevant even today.

Reagan faced the same kind of political opposition we conservatives face today.

And his response captures the core truth we must remember: that it is our opponents who are the extremists, not us. As he said:

Let us lay to rest, once and for all, the myth [that conservatives are] a small group of ideological purists trying to capture a majority. Replace it with the reality of a majority trying to assert its rights against the tyranny of powerful academics, fashionable left-revolutionaries, some economic illiterates who happen to hold elective office and the social engineers who dominate the dialogue and set the format in political and social affairs. If there is any ideological fanaticism in American political life, it is to be found among the enemies of freedom on the left or right—those who would sacrifice principle to theory, those who worship only the god of political, social and economic abstractions, ignoring the realities of everyday life. They are not conservatives.[12]

TEN

ITEMS FOR VICTORY

In April 2007, I first published a list on Hannity.com that I called Top 10 Items for Victory. In the list—which I'll expand upon in these final pages—I set down what strike me as the most important policy points conservatives must focus on in the coming years. It's not an exhaustive list, but each of the items on it is an essential part of the conservative agenda. Together they offer a primer on the key tenets around which the new Republican Party must unite—both as a matter of conservative principle and to maximize its chances for victory in 2010 and 2012.

By no means do I intend the items as a new Contract with America that congressional candidates must endorse or sign. But they do point up the principles upon which I believe any such contract should be based. Of course, not every one of the principles I'm presenting here calls for federal legislation. But as we saw in chapter 8, the original Contract with America was quite specific in the legislative items it promised to draft and bring to the floor of the House, and any future contract based on the principles I'm setting out should be equally specific in order to ensure accountability of those legislators and candidates who sign it. I'll leave the drafting of any such contract to those more equipped for the legislative and drafting process. But I cannot say strongly enough that, as a party, we must return to the following general principles, rally around them, and focus our united efforts on achieving them.

Our electoral success depends on it.

1. NATIONAL SECURITY

The 2008 Republican National Committee's party platform issued a clear warning about the dangers of an "amateur foreign policy" characterized by the "wreckage of inexperienced good intentions at the highest levels of government." As part of our governing philosophy, unlike our major opposition, we recognize that there are both good and evil forces in the world, and that we must confront evil, instead of appeasing and accommodating it.

On this issue more than any other, except for fiscal policy, Republicans must draw clear and sharp distinctions between ourselves and our opponents, who have taken every possible opportunity to undermine our national security. We must remind voters of what Democrats stand for—and of how easily those beliefs can become policy when they control both the executive and the legislative branches of our government. On nearly every issue since the war on terror began, Democrats have stood for the wrong principles and policies and have proved incompetent in carrying out their own policies as well. As soon as the dust of 9/11 lifted, they broke allegiance with their government in a time of war—while cloaking their antimilitary message in policy nuance, hoping to create the impression that they merely

disagreed with Bush's focus and methods in the war. They undermined our intelligence operations but claimed to be doing so in
deference to our civil liberties. They reverted to the Clinton-era
position of treating the war as a criminal prosecution, replete
with constitutional protections for enemy combatants, and replaced what should have been military tribunals held outside the
mainland with trials in U.S. civilian courts.

Democrats continue to apologize for America, what it stands
for, and its unique record of prosperity. By contrast, we must
make clear to the American voter that we are proud of America,
and that we love the military, the flag, the Pledge of Allegiance,
and America's history of benevolence toward the international
community. Never in history has a nation—let alone the world's
sole superpower—been so magnanimous, so generous with its
resources, so humane toward other peoples; we are not the arrogant imperialist nation Obama and his party have portrayed.
Though we have long since possessed the power and resources
to conquer the world, when we have intervened in foreign skir-
mishes, conflicts, and wars it has largely been to protect our national interests or the democratic interests of oppressed peoples.

We should make clear that we believe that a strong military,
and cutting-edge weapons and technology, are essential to preserving the peace. The concept of "peace through strength" may
be difficult for our liberal friends to grasp, but it makes perfect
sense to most Americans, and we consider it a guiding principle of
sound foreign policy. It was Ronald Reagan's steadfast insistence
on SDI in Reykjavik, against the hysterical hand-wringing of
nuclear freeze liberals, that eventually forced Mikhail Gorbachev
to capitulate in the Cold War. We won not by surrendering, but
by protecting our interests and our principles from a position of
strength. We must continue in that tradition as the party that

promotes peace through strength as a means of preserving our unique liberties and security.

As such, we must be committed to retaining our position as the world's greatest superpower, by maintaining the world's strongest military and supporting our troops on and off the battlefield. We must not dismantle our nuclear weapons and must persist in perfecting our strategic missile defense systems. We must oppose the acquisition of nuclear weapons by Iran and other rogue regimes.

We must make clear that we are in a protracted war against radical Islamists, and against those nation states that sponsor or aid them—not because we have something against Islamists, but because they are at war with us, whether some refuse to recognize it or not. They are not at war with us because we mistreat prisoners or are wealthy; they are at war with us because we don't share their warped ideology and theology. We must fight this war aggressively, resisting the temptation to treat it as a matter for law enforcement.

We must, however, be clear that we aren't warmongers, but in fact reluctant warriors who believe we must win the war in order to preserve our liberties and our way of life. Our leaders must make clear that, unlike the opposition party, we are not nationally suicidal idealists who insist we can end animosities between the West and radical Islamists by changing *our* behavior. Rather, we are realists who recognize the world as it truly is, even when that means defying the hallowed precepts of political correctness. As realists, we know that we must approach the world's dangerous and corrupt tyrants as if they are dangerous and corrupt tyrants. They probably won't like us, but they *must* respect us. We will not negotiate with terrorists or the regimes that sponsor them, without preconditions.

We must promote our international alliances, not by conforming to the misguided progressive notions of leftist leaders but by acting humanely and in our national interests. We must encourage and support—even if at times it can only be moral support—prodemocratic movements throughout the world, when it is not inconsistent with our national interests.

We must preserve our victory in Iraq and seek to stabilize that nation as a burgeoning democracy, and, hopefully, a catalyst for other democratic movements in the Middle East. We must continue to fight the Taliban in Afghanistan as long as it is feasible, and as long as Afghanistan remains a hotbed for terrorist recruitment, support, and training.

Above all, we must wage a multifaceted, aggressive war against the global jihadists—and I did say "global." Our enemy, no matter how much Democrats wish it were otherwise, is not just Al Qaeda. We must commit whatever resources are necessary to wage this war, do everything necessary to strengthen and coordinate our intelligence services (including vital information sharing), and protect legislation, such as the Patriot Act, that is designed to enhance our security, always careful to maintain that important balance between national security and our individual liberties.

2. ECONOMIC GROWTH AND FISCAL RESPONSIBILITY

We must be the party of growth and fiscal responsibility. This means supporting reduced marginal income taxes, including capital gains taxes; the elimination of the estate tax; the elimination of earmarks; drastically reducing and capping discretionary domestic spending; and the good-faith pursuit of balanced budgets. Nothing stifles economic growth and prosperity like our onerous tax structure. Nothing threatens our future as a nation of liberty like the current administration's fiscal policies—and entitlements. Our candidates must communicate that tax policy and revenues are not a zero-sum game; that lower tax rates can generate more revenues; and that "a rising tide lifts all boats" is not a phony platitude but actually a proven historical fact. By lowering the tax and regulatory burden on individuals and businesses, we will unleash once again the full force and energy of the free market, generating greater prosperity and promoting fiscal stability.

3. ENERGY INDEPENDENCE

We must support "energy independence," including the immediate lifting of bans against:

A. Drilling in the Alaska National Wildlife Refuge and the forty-eight states, on- and off-shore
B. Building new refineries
C. Building and using nuclear facilities
D. Expanding coal mining

We should make the case that we are responsible stewards of the environment and will encourage the government to work with private industry to develop new energy technologies, with the goal that America achieve energy independence within the next fifteen years.

4. IMMIGRATION

Our party must adopt a responsible, balanced immigration policy that honors the rule of law, with its candidates pledging to secure our borders completely within twelve months by:

A. Building all necessary fences
B. Using all available technology to help and support agents at the border
C. Hiring and training all border agents necessary to accomplish these goals

5. HEALTH CARE

We must communicate that the problems in our health-care system—especially its soaring costs—are largely due to government laws and regulations that have interfered with market forces. Our leaders should promote a series of solutions designed to restore market forces to the industry, including:

A. Reversing tax laws that discriminate between employer-provided insurance and individually acquired insurance—laws that have made prices and costs "invisible" to the consumer, thus guaranteeing their escalation
B. Expanding the availability of health savings accounts
C. Implementing tort reform legislation
D. Eliminating government-imposed coverage mandates that are driving up costs
E. Deregulating the market to eliminate restrictions on the interstate purchasing of policies, in order to

increase competition and choice in the market and
lower costs
F. Promoting the idea that health insurance coverage
should be used to pay for catastrophic health expenses,
not routine checkups or treatment of minor ailments

6. EDUCATION

We must support rescuing children from our government-
imposed education system, which is failing our children and our
nation. Our candidates should:

A. Support choice in education, including vouchers
to parents to level the playing field between public
and private educational institutions, thus encouraging the pursuit of excellence in each system through
increased competition and accountability
B. Fight the unholy alliance between the Democratic
Party and the NEA, a relationship that has institu-
tionalized mediocrity and prioritized liberal indoctrination above the academic education of our students

7. ENTITLEMENT REFORM

When it suited the Democrats' political interests, they pretended
to agree with conservatives that we were facing a looming fiscal
crisis with Social Security and other entitlements. Bill Clinton and
Al Gore sensationalized the issue, going so far as to recommend
a "lock box" for social security revenues. When George W. Bush
tried to reform Social Security, though, the Democrats fell back
on their familiar scare tactics, accusing Republicans of jeopardiz-

ing the retirement funds of America's senior citizens and denying there was a crisis at all. With the current economic slowdown, however, the imminent insolvency of our entitlement programs is no longer debatable. The *Wall Street Journal* has reported that that the government has recently revised its estimates for the long-term solvency of Medicare and Social Security, with Medicare running a deficit for the first time last year, and the Social Security fund to be exhausted in 2037, four years earlier than previously estimated.[1] As such, the GOP must support responsible entitlement reform, designed to preserve reasonable benefits without bankrupting our children's and grandchildren's futures. Our candidates must have the courage to support a private component in their reform legislation, without which it will be much more difficult to restore long-term solvency to the programs.

8. LAW AND ORDER

We must retain our party's position as the preeminent defender of law enforcement, recognizing that one of the few, but essential, functions of government is to establish and maintain law and order. We must promote criminal legislation designed to maximize law and order without sacrificing the constitutional rights of our citizens, including those accused of crimes. With that in mind, we must support the appointment of judges who interpret the Constitution according to its original intent—that is, what the framers actually meant when they drafted it—and who interpret legislation according to the historically established rules of statutory construction, as opposed to judges who legislate from the bench and create new constitutional rights out of whole cloth. We must support and protect our law enforcement officers.

9. SECOND AMENDMENT

We must endorse and defend, without apology, the right of the people—and that means individuals—to keep and bear arms for self-protection and self-defense. We must counter the disinformation that private gun ownership and possession cost more lives than they save. We must affirm our belief in holding criminals accountable through enforcement of federal and state firearms laws, but oppose onerous gun control laws and regulations, and frivolous lawsuits against firearms manufacturers designed to dilute our Second Amendment rights.

10. SOCIAL AND VALUES ISSUES

As much as any other issue, we must be the party that honors and champions the sanctity of human life. We must vigorously protect the life of the unborn, and oppose embryonic stem cell research and cloning.

We must stand for preserving traditional marriage and oppose efforts to legalize same-sex marriage.

We must be the party that protects religious liberties—which means opposing the efforts of secularists to suppress religious freedoms under a highly exaggerated and distorted notion of church-state separation. There are two religious freedom clauses in the First Amendment: the free exercise clause and the establishment clause. We must oppose efforts to smother the free exercise clause in service to an unduly expansive notion of the establishment clause. There is nothing harmful or illegal about recitation of the Pledge of Allegiance in public schools. There is nothing in the Constitution that forbids voluntary prayer in public schools. Cliched though it may sound, we believe in freedom *of* religion, not freedom *from* religion.

We must be the party that stands for equal treatment of all individuals under law and promotes racial and ethnic color-blindness. We must oppose discrimination, including that involved in quotas, set-asides, and other forms of affirmative action, recognizing that such programs harm, not promote, the dignity of individuals—all of whom are created in God's image.

We must be the party that prides itself on its patriotic love for America and stands for American exceptionalism.

Finally, on the issue of values, we must be the party that recaptures its image of putting forth candidates of character and integrity and which governs with true transparency, as distinguished from President Obama's false promises for openness in government. Also, we should fulfill two other promises that Obama made, but breached:

1. To eliminate the revolving door between lobbying and governance so as to drastically reduce conflicts of interest that would otherwise arise.

2. To publish proposed bills on the Internet days in advance of their consideration by either chamber, in keeping with our strong belief that honesty in government is nonnegotiable, and with confidence that our policies are in the mainstream of American thought. We must never allow our pride to lead us to believe that we are infallible and above the need for direct accountability to the people.

11. THE CONSTITUTION

Our party must be known far and wide as the party that is committed to constitutional government. This means respecting the United States Constitution as written and according to its original intent. As such our candidates will honor the structure of government established by the Constitution, including the concept of federalism that divides power between the state and local governments; full and robust states' rights, as guaranteed by the Tenth Amendment and otherwise in the body of the document; the separation of powers between three coequal branches of government and enforced by a scheme of checks and balances; a judiciary that interprets rather than makes laws; and executive and legislative branches that honor these concepts. Our candidates must promise to appoint and/or confirm only judges who subscribe to an originalist judicial philosophy.

Our party must also stand for and promote America's national sovereignty and must oppose efforts to subordinate our sovereignty to international bodies. We must support the appointment and confirmation of judges who, as originalists, reject the notion of transnationalism, which places the laws of other nations that have not been affirmed through our treaty-making authority on par with laws of the United States.

12. AMERICAN DREAM, FREE ENTERPRISE, PRIVATE PROPERTY, LIBERTY

As the party loyal to the Constitution as written, we must continue to make the case that our constitution, along with our Judeo-Christian values, is the primary reason we enjoy greater liberties than any other nation in history—liberties that are inalienably bestowed upon us by God. Thus, we must adhere to the notion that the primary role of the federal government is to preserve, protect, and defend those liberties. Our party and its candidates must endorse our belief in private enterprise, free-market capitalism, personal responsibility, ordered liberty, and the rule of law. We should promote rugged individualism and personal responsibility and the idea that, in the words of Abraham Lincoln, the United States is "the last, best hope of earth," and that our best days are before us—if our government will simply trust the American people.

ACKNOWLEDGMENTS

I always thank God for the many blessings in my life, including my health, my family, and the endless opportunities I have received. My faith grows stronger every day as I realize that God's plan is what matters, not the myopic thoughts, dreams, or goals of one fallen soul.

This book was inspired by all the people who write me; by my callers; by people like those I met on April 15, 2009, in Atlanta and at the other Tea Party events and town halls throughout 2009. Your unwavering commitment to the cause of freedom made me realize we all have to work to get the country we love back on track, not necessarily for ourselves, but for our children and grandchildren. Thank you for what you do every day—your voices are having a HUGE impact, and you offer us great hope for the future.

Thanks to David Limbaugh, author, syndicated columnist, and my agent and attorney, who has been there for me from day one, and continues to be an enormous blessing in my life. He was the principal editor of this book, and his insights and contributions made it dramatically better than it otherwise would have been. I would also like to thank David's brother Rush, America's # 1 talk show host, who first gave me national radio exposure by letting me fill in on his program. There is no greater patriot or friend than Rush. I cannot imagine a USA without these two great Americans named Limbaugh.

To the Great One, Mark Levin: It was during one of our frequent late-night conversations that he convinced me this book could help advance our shared conservative agenda. Our daily discussions crystallized for me the need to lay out, in detail, why victory is imperative, and how the principles of history apply to today's challenges.

To Roger Ailes, my boss at the Fox News Channel: My first few months on Fox were shaky at best, and Roger had every right to fire me—but instead he worked with me patiently, giving me the time I needed to grow while always allowing me to be myself. Roger is by far the smartest, quickest, and funniest person I know, and many of the great things in my life grew directly out of his taking a chance on me in October 1996, and his sticking by me ever since. Roger, I can never thank you enough.

Bill Shine, one of my closest friends, is there for me daily. My rule in life is, *Always listen to Shine.* I have learned from experience that he's never wrong; he offers me sound counsel and daily support. Few people in TV have his innate talents, and few work as hard—and he does so with grace and a smile at all times. Thank you, Bill—and Darla!

Also at Fox: Thanks to Suzanne Scott, whose endless support and creative input makes every day a pleasure. Few people are as passionate and competitive. And thanks to the rest of my television team, led by my executive producer John Finley, better known as "Skippy," a term of endearment I use when he's mad at me. John grinds out shows and ideas on a daily basis; he is a true creative genius. And thanks to an extraordinary staff: my assistant, Elise Sabbeth, who keeps my schedule sane; and Paulina, Meghan, Tim, Dan, Tara, Jennie, Kathryn, Chris, Eliana, Chase, Lauren, Tiffany, Caitlin. A special thank you to my sister-in-law Emily Rhodes, an artistic genius who does great graphic work for the Fox News Channel, for her creative design input on the cover of this book. I also have to thank the best director in television, Chet Lishawa, and the entire behind-the-scenes production team at Fox—from the hair and makeup people, to the set crew, cameras, lighting, sound, and Teleprompter. They make every day fun—especially when we're throwing the football around.

I also need to thank Dianne Brandi in the Fox legal department for her tireless and incredibly loyal support. The same goes for Brian Lewis and Irena Briganti and their team running the Fox News Channel PR department: There are no greater people to have in your corner when you're under fire.

To friends from Premiere Radio: CEO John Hogan, a dear friend who believed in me from our earliest days together in Atlanta. Julie Talbott, Charlie Rahilly, Dan Meter, Eric Stanger (the "Stanganator"), who keep everything running smoothly. To sweet baby James, who is like a brother to me. To Elisha, Lynda, Eileen, Greg, and Blair, who make it all happen every day. (I'm purposefully omitting their last names because certain members of my radio team fear their exposure could result in an Obama administration tax audit.) To Scott Shannon, the "VOICE" of *The Sean Hannity Show* and one of the most gifted talents in radio history. Scott is the one guy who will let me know, on a regular basis, how I can improve.

From Citadel Broadcasting: CEO Farid Suleman, also a dear friend and a terrific support. Steve Bornemen and Laurie Cantillo of WABC, my flagship radio station, whose support is unwavering. I would be negligent if I didn't mention Phil Boyce, my former PD at WABC, who encouraged me to take the show national and was from the beginning a true force in the show's development.

Sean Compton at Tribune, whose passion for talk radio is second to none—your wise counsel is always appreciated. Other close friends in radio, such as Bob Michaels, Greg Moceri, and Mark Masters, who are always there helping me be better. And a very special thank you to all of my affiliate stations and their GMs and PDs, who allow me to do what I love every day.

To my personal friends John Gomez (Congressman Gomez one day?), who has been there with me since third grade, and Dave Stone, Bill Dunnavant, and Eric Seidel, who believed in me early and are still dear friends today.

I have to also thank the people who are instrumental in pulling off our annual Freedom Concert tours: Col. Oliver North, a true American hero; Duane Ward from PremiereSpeakers.com, the guy who gets it done; and Frank Breeden and Tom Kilgannon of the Freedom Alliance scholarship fund, the charity that provides college scholarships for the children of military heroes who have lost their lives or are permanently disabled.

Calvert Morgan, my editor at HarperCollins, has worked on all three of my books; there is no one better in the industry. Cal, you make it easy.

I am most grateful for the support of my family, the greatest blessing and joy in my life: My wife, Jill; my son, Patrick; and my daughter, Merri Kelly. They make every day worthwhile. Also for my sisters, Mary-Jo and Therese; their husbands, Steve and James; and my nieces and nephews—when they're NOT in trouble—Cassandra, Brandon, Michael, Sarah, and Christopher. I appreciate everybody for making my life what it is today, and for making this book possible.

Finally, a special thank you to YOU, the audience. Without you listening to the radio show and watching *Hannity*, none of this would be possible. I can never thank you enough.

NOTES

CHAPTER ONE

1 Ronald Reagan, "We Will Be As a City upon a Hill," Conservative Political Action Conference, Washington, D.C., January 25, 1974.

2 Transcript, *Face the Nation* (CBS News), Interview with John Kerry, Sunday, December 4, 2005.

3 Rowan Scarborough, "Gitmo Called Death Camp," *Washington Times,* June 15, 2005.

4 James Traub, "The Counterinsurgent," *New York Times,* October 5, 2008.

5 Kara Rowland, "Critics Not Invited to White House Jobs Summit," *Washington Times,* December 2, 2010.

6 Kara Rowland, "Obama Wants to Use TARP for New Jobs Bill, McCain Says President Can't," *Washington Times*, December 9, 2009.

7 Scott Rasmussen, "Health Reform and the Polls, Obama's biggest obstacle is the 68% of voters who rate their health coverage as good or excellent," Opinion Journal, *Wall Street Journal,* August 7, 2009.

8 Bill Sammon, "Obama's 47 Percent Approval Lowest of Any President at This Point," FoxNews.com, December 8, 2009.

9 Erik Rush, "Obamination," Howardwasright.com, February 21, 2007.

10 Manya A. Brachear and Bob Secter, "Race is Sensitive Subtext in Campaign; South Side Church's Tenets Spark Criticism of Obama by Some Conservatives," *Chicago Tribune,* February 6, 2007.

11 Transcript, "Questions Raised About Obama's Church," Fox News Channel, February 28, 2007.

12 Jodi Kantor, "A Candidate, His Minister and the Search for Faith," *New York Times,* April 30, 2007.

13 Paul Enns, *The Moody Handbook of Theology* (Chicago: Moody, 1989), pp. 599–600.

14 Kyle-Anne Shiver, "Obama, Black Liberation Theology, and Karl Marx," *American Thinker*, December 10, 2009.

15 James H. Cone, *A Black Theology of Liberation* (Philadelphia and New York: Lippincott, 1970), p. 70.

16 Ibid., p. 38.

17 James H. Cone, *Black Theology and Black Power* (New York: Harper & Row, 1997), p. 31.

18 Cone, *A Black Theology of Liberation*, p. 5.

19 Cone, *Black Theology and Black Power*, p. 130.

20 Ibid., p. 120; Cone, *A Black Theology of Liberation*, p. 10.

21 Cone, *Black Theology and Black Power*, p. viii.

22 John S. Feinberg, *No One Like Him* (Wheaton, Ill.: Crossway, 2001), p. 130.

23 Ronald Kessler, "Barack Obama's Racist Church," Newsmax.com, January 7, 2008.

24 Ben Wallace-Wells, "Destiny's Child," *Rolling Stone*, February 22, 2007.

25 Brian Ross and Rehab El-buri, "Obama's Pastor: God Damn America, U.S. to Blame for 9/11," Brian Ross, "The Blotter," ABCNews.go.com, March 13, 2008.

26 Ibid.

27 Mike Glover, "Obama Says He's Outraged by Former Pastor's Comments," Associated Press, April 29, 2008.

28 John McCormack, "Not the Same Rev. Wright?" The Blog, WeeklyStandard .com, April 29, 2008.

29 Kantor, "A Candidate, His Minister and the Search for Faith."

30 Ibid.

31 Barack Obama, "Obama Audacity of Hope Speech Inspired by His Pastor," YouTube Video, undated, http://noolmusic.com/youtube_videos/obama_audacity _of_hope_speech_inspired_by_his_pastor.php.

32 Ben Wallace-Wells, "Destiny's Child," *Rolling Stone*, February 22, 2007.

33 Barack Obama, *Dreams from My Father* (New York: Crown, 1995), p. xv.

34 Wallace-Wells, "Destiny's Child."

35 Andrew Walden, "Barack Obama: Red Diaper Baby," *American Thinker*, October 30, 2008.

36 Tim Jones, "Family Portraits: Strong Personalities Shaped a Future Senator, Barack Obama," *Chicago Tribune*, March 27, 2007.

37 James Lewis, "Obama the Red Avenger," *American Thinker*, December 15, 2009.

38 Walden, "Barack Obama: Red Diaper Baby."

39 Ibid.

40 Ibid.

41 Ibid.

42 Tim Jones, "Barack Obama: Mother Not Just a Girl from Kansas," *Chicago Tribune,* March 27, 2007.

43 Lewis, "Obama the Red Avenger."

44 David Fredosso, *The Case Against Barack Obama* (Washington, D.C. Regnery, 2008), p. 122.

45 L. David Alinsky, "Son Sees Father's Handiwork in Convention," *Boston Globe,* August 31, 2008.

46 Cliff Kincaid, "Obama's Communist Mentor," Accuracy in Media, February 18, 2008.

47 Stanley Kurtz, "Obama and Ayers Pushed Radicalism On Schools," *Wall Street Journal,* September 23, 2008.

48 Dinitia Smith, "No Regrets for a Love of Explosives; In a Memoir of Sorts, a War Protestor Talks of Life With the Weathermen," *New York Times,* September 11, 2001.

49 Ibid.

50 Ibid.

51 Kurtz, "Obama and Ayers Pushed Radicalism On Schools."

52 Clif Kincaid, "Obama's International Socialist Connections," Accuracy in Media, February 14, 2008.

53 Spengler, "Obama's Women Reveal His Secret," *Asia Times,* February 26, 2008.

54 Michelle Obama: "For the First Time In My Adult Lifetime, I Am Really Proud of My Country," BreitbartTV, February 29, 2008; "Michelle Obama Takes Heat for Saying She's 'Proud of My Country,' " FoxNews.com, February 19, 2008.

CHAPTER TWO

1 Editorial, "Eye on the Prize," CPUSA.org, July, 15, 2008.

2 Testimony of William Frapolly, The Chicago Seven Trial, http://www.law.umkc .edu/faculty/projects/ftrials/Chicago7/Frapolly.html.

3 Guy Benson, "Obama's Radical Delegate," Townhall.com, August 31, 2008.

4 Ibid.

5 Jeff Zeleny, "President's Political Protector Is Ever Close at Hand," *New York Times,* March 8, 2009.

6 Patrick T. Reardon, "The Agony and the Agony: Renowned Political Guru David Axelrod Can Cap his Career by Helping Barack Obama Win the White House. But Will It Calm the Forces Driving Him?" *Chicago Tribune,* June 24, 2007.

7 "Axelrod's Communist Associations," AIPNews.com, September 11, 2009.

8 Marc Canter, "My Family Has Been Outed—We're Dam Commies—But We Aren't Paid to Be," Marc's Voice, November 3, 2008, http://blog.broadband

mechanics.com/2008/11/03/my-family-has-been-outed-were-dam-commies -but-we-aint-paid-to-be/.

9 Ben Johnson, "Valerie Jarrett: The Next Van Jones," FrontPageMagazine.com, September 14, 2009.

10 "Valerie Jarrett: The Other Side of Obama's Brain," Huffington Post, August 12, 2008.

11 Robert Draper, "The Ultimate Obama Insider," *New York Times,* July 26, 2009.

12 http://www.youtube.com/watch?v=Ud_yNFnfrSI.

13 Laurie Cohen and Ray Gibson, "Plugged into City's Power," *Chicago Tribune,* November 21, 2008.

14 The Prowler, "Who is Valerie Jarrett?" *American Spectator,* August 26, 2008.

15 Binyamin Appelbaum, "Grim Proving Ground for Obama's Housing Policy," *Boston Globe,* June 27, 2008.

16 Robert Draper, "The Ultimate Obama Insider," *New York Times Magazine,* July 21, 2009.

17 Seton Motley, "Video: FCC 'Diversity' Czar on Chavez's Venezuela: 'Incredible . . . Democratic Revolution,' " NewsBusters.org, August 28, 2009.

18 Ibid.

19 Associated Press, "Venezuela Sets New Restrictions on Cable TV," *New York Times,* July 9, 2009.

20 Juan O. Tamayo, "Report: Venezuela's Hugo Chavez Aggressively Seizing Control of Media," *Miami Herald,* August 14, 2009.

21 Kyle Smith, "Gag the Internet! An Obama Official's Frightening Book About Curbing Free Speech Online," *New York Post,* July 11, 2009.

22 Cass R. Sunstein and Richard H. Thaler, "Libertarian Paternalism Is Not an Oxymoron," *University of Chicago Law Review,* April 3, 2003.

23 Cass Sunstein and Martha Nussbaum, *Animal Rights: Current Debates and New Directions* (New York: Oxford University Press, 2004), [p. TK].

24 Richard Neuhaus, "While We're At It; The Public Square: A Continuing Survey of Religion and Public Life"; Various Items, *First Things: A Monthly Journal of Religion and Public Life,* November 1, 2002.

25 "Cass Sunstein: Facts and Talking Points," Eagle Forum, 2009.

26 "Obama Expands Car Czar's Duties, Ron Bloom to Work on Boosting U.S. Competitiveness in Manufacturing," *Washington Post,* September 8, 2009.

27 Andrea Tantaros, "Anita Dunn and the Obama White House: Outfoxed," FoxNews.com, November 10, 2009.

28 Byron York, "Why Did the Press Ignore the Van Jones Scandal?" *Washington Examiner,* September 8, 2009.

29 Eliza Strickland, "The New Face of Environmentalism," *East Bay Express,* November 2, 2005.

30 Byron York, "Obama Stands by Kevin Jennings—Or Does He?" *Washington Examiner,* October 11, 2009.

31 Jim Hoft, "Breaking: Obama's 'Safe Schools Czar; Is Promoting Child Porn in the Classroom—Kevin Jennings and the GLSEN Reading List," GatewayPundit .firstthings.com, December 4, 2009. See also http://www.orthodoxytoday .org/blog/2009/12/08/obamas-safe-schools-czar-promotes-child-porn-in-the -classroom-kevin-jenningss-glsen-reading-list/.

32 Byron York, "Lawmaker Calls on Obama to Fire Official in Gay Sex Ed Controversy," *Washington Examiner,* October 5, 2009.

33 Ibid.

34 Fred Lucas, "Obama's Christian Appointee to Faith-Based Program Says New Testament Teaching on Homosexuality Is 'Not True,' " CNSNews.com, April 8, 2009.

35 Editorial, "Browner Is an Environmental Radical—and a Socialist (Seriously)," *Washington Examiner,* January 8, 2009.

36 Stephen Dinan, "Obama Climate Czar Has Socialist Ties, Group sees 'global governance' as solution," *Washington Times,* January 12, 2009.

37 David Freddoso, "Obama's Science Czar Suggested Compulsory Abortion, Sterilization," *Washington Examiner,* July 14, 2009.

38 Michelle Malkin, "The Science Czar Stonewalls," MichelleMalkin.com, July 21, 2009.

39 Pete Winn, "Sebelius Likely to Defer to Congressional Dems in Crafting Health Care Reform Bill," CNSNews.com, March 3, 2009.

40 Ibid.

41 David Usborne, "Shooting of US Abortion Doctor Shocks Obama," *The Independent* (UK), June 1, 2009.

42 Hans Nichols, "Obama Names Yale Law Dean to State Department Post (Update 2)," Bloomberg.com, March 23, 2009.

43 Andrew McCarthy, "I Have 'Shocked' OLC Nominee Dawn Johnsen," The Corner, National Review Online, February 26, 2009.

44 Andrew McCarthy, "Lawyer's Lawyer, Radical's Radical," *National Review,* March 9, 2009.

45 Steven Ertelt, "President Obama Makes First Pro-Abortion Judicial Pick in David Hamilton," LifeNews.com, March 17, 2009.

46 Rosa Brooks, "A Really Bad Case of 'Reality,' " *Los Angeles Times,* July 20, 2007.

47 Aaron Klein, "Pentagon Official Blames U.S. for Al-Qaida Attacks, Worked for George Soros, Argued for Government Control of Media," WorldNetDaily .com, April 20, 2009.

48 Jonathan Martin, "Code-Pink Co-Founder is Obama Bundler," Politico.com, June 11, 2008.

49 Kristinn Taylor and Andrea Shea King, "Jane Fonda: Obama Funder Jodie Evans Met With Taliban; Code Pink Gives Terrorists Direct Line to Obama," BigGovernment.com, November 17, 2009; Jane Fonda, "Armand Hammer Museum," http://janefonda.com/armand-hammer-museum.

50 Kristinn Taylor and Andrea Shea King, "Obama Funder Jodie Evans and Her New 'Tali' Pals: Taliban Brings Peace and Justice, U.S. Created 'Hell on Earth' in Afghanistan," BigGovernment.com, December 21, 2009.

51 Kristinn Taylor and Andrea Shea King, "Obama Funder 'Jodie Evans' in White House Visitor Log days after Code Pink Hamas Trip," BigGovernment.com, January 8, 2010.

52 Richard Baehr and Ed Lasky, "Samantha Power and Obama's Foreign Policy Team," *American Thinker*, February 19, 2008.

53 Joseph Klein, "Saved from Durban II," FrontPageMagazine.com, March 2, 2009.

54 Richard Baehr and Ed Lasky, "Samantha Power and Obama's Foreign Policy Team," *American Thinker*, February 19, 2008.

55 Robert Costa, "Unrepealable?" The Corner, National Review Online, December 22, 2009.

CHAPTER THREE

1 Brian M. Riedl, "The Obama Budget: Spending, Taxes, and Doubling the National Debt, at FN7" Heritage.org, March 16, 2009.

2 Transcript, "Transcript: Obama and Clinton Debate," ABCNews.com, April 16, 2008.

3 Michael Goodwin, "Obama's Search for an Enemy: The President keep beating the class warfare drum," New York *Daily News*, March 7, 2009.

4 "Obama vs. the Washington Establishment," *Washington Post*, February 28, 2009.

5 Kyle Trygstad and Mike Memoli, "Obama: 'Now is Not the Time' For Excessive Bonuses," Politics Nation, January 29, 2009.

6 Jeff Poor, "Cramer on Obama's Anti-Wall Street Comments: 'We Heard Levin,' 'Mad Money' Host Compares New President's Attack on Corporate Profits to Rhetoric from Russian Communist," Business and Media Institute, February 2, 2009.

7 Editorial, "A 40-Year Wish List," *Wall Street Journal*, January 28, 2009.

8 News Release, "Harvard Economics Professor Calls Stimulus 'Terrible Piece of Legislation,' " Tax Foundation, February 19, 2009.

9 Brian M. Riedl, "The Obama Budget: Spending, Taxes, and Doubling the National Debt," Heritage.org, March 16, 2009.

10 Mark Impomeni, "Obama to Break Campaign Promise, Sign Earmark-Laden Spending Bill," *Politics Daily*, March 2, 2009.

11 Walter Alarkon, "Obama Falls Short on Pledge To Curtail Earmarks, Fiscal Hawks Say," *The Hill*, December 26, 2009.

12 "Transcript of Second McCain, Obama Debate," CNNPolitics.com, October 7, 2008.

13 Brian M. Riedl, "Obama's Budget Seeks $2 Trillion More in Spending and Deficits than Last Year," Heritage Foundation, WebMemo #2787, February 1, 2010.

14 Ibid.

15 Ibid.

16 Walter Alarkon, "Budget Request Projects $1.56 Trillion Deficit," *The Hill*, February 1, 2010.

17 Brian M. Riedl, "WebMemo #2595, "New Budget Estimates Show Unsustainable Spending and Debt, Heritage.org, August 25, 2009.

18 Ibid.

19 Phil Rosenthal, "Rant by CNBC's Rick Santelli Puts Pundit at Odds with Obama Administration," *Chicago Tribune,* February 22, 2009.

20 Victoria McGrane, "White House's $50B Foreclosure Plan a Bust So Far," Politico.com, July 17, 2009.

21 Ibid.

22 Shahien Nasiripour, "Bailout Watchdog: Obama Foreclosure Plan Inadequate, New Plan Needed," Huffington Post, December 9, 2009.

23 "December Oversight Report, Taking Stock: What Has the Troubled Asset Relief Program Achieved?" Congressional Oversight Panel, December 9, 2009.

24 Tami Luhby, "30,383: First Tally on Stimulus Jobs," October 15, 2009.

25 Rea S. Hedermen, Jr., and James Sherk, WebMemo #2685, "Heritage Employment Report: October Has Few Treats, Lots of Tricks," Heritage.org, November 6, 2009.

26 Andrea Tantaros, "President Obama's Jobs Summit is a Great Feast of Folly," New York *Daily News,* December 3, 2009.

27 Associated Press, "Newspaper: Stimulus Brings Few Private-Sector Jobs," November 15, 2009.

28 Fred Lucas, "Recovery.gov Shows Taxpayer Money Going to Congressional Districts That Don't Exist," CNSNews.com, November 18, 2009.

29 Jim Scarantino, "Stimulus Funds Went to Nonexistent Zip Code Areas," New Mexico Watchdog, NewMexico.Watchdog.org, January 3, 2010.

30 Thomas Peele and Josh Richman, "Stimulus Money Pouring into Bay Area," *Oakland Tribune,* January 3, 2010.

31 Mona Charen, "Democratic Payoffs, Er, Stimulus," Townhall.com, January 5, 2010.

32 Brian M. Riedl, "Why Government Spending Does Not Stimulate Economic Growth: Answering the Critics," Backgrounder #2354, Heritage Foundation, January 5, 2010.

33 Terrence P. Jeffery, "Despite Obama's Repeated Claims That Enacting $787 Billion Stimulus Was Urgent, 78 Percent of Money Remained Unspent by End of Fiscal 2009 Says Federal Auditing Agency," November 23, 2009.

34 Andrew Taylor, "Obama Pins Hope for Job Creation on Jobs Plan," CNSNews .com, December 4, 2009.

35 Christopher Neefus, "As Obama Pushes for Second Stimulus, Federal Audit Says States Have Only Spent One-Quarter of Funds Set Aside for Them in First Stimulus," CNSNews.com, December 16, 2009.

36 Declan McCullagh, "EPA May Have Suppressed Report Skeptical of Global Warming," Political Hotsheet, CBS News, June 26, 2009.

37 Charlie Martin, "Fast Facts About Climategate," Pajamasmedia.com, December 6, 2009.

38 Marc Sheppard, "Understanding Climategate's Hidden Decline," American Thinker, December 6, 2009; Charlie Martin, "Fast Facts About Climategate," Pajamasmedia.com, December 6, 2009.

39 Opinion, "Climate of Uncertainty Heats Up, Bloggers Peer Review a Scientific 'Consensus,' " OpinionJournal.com, Wall Street Journal, December 6, 2009.

40 Kerry Picket, "Obama: Energy Prices Will Skyrocket Under My Cap and Trade Plan," NewsBusters.org, November 2, 2008.

41 Ben Lieberman, "The Waxman-Markey Global Warming Bill: Is the Economic Pain Justified by the Environmental Gain?" Heritage.org, June 23, 2009.

42 Ibid.

43 Editorial, "Five Decades of Cooling Ahead," Investors.com, December 24, 2009.

44 "Democrats Could Learn From LBJ's Medicare Push," National Public Radio, August 26, 2009, http://www.npr.org/templates/story/story.php?storyId=112234240.

45 Scott Rasmussen, "Health Reform and the Polls, Obama's Biggest Obstacle is the 68% of Voters Who Rate Their Health Coverage as Good or Excellent," Opinion Journal, Wall Street Journal, August 7, 2009.

46 Rasmussen Reports, "Health Care Reform, Health Care Legislation Advancing in Senate, Stalled in Public Opinion," December 21, 2009.

47 Rasmussen Reports, "Obama Approval Index History," Rasmussenreports.com.

48 Rasmussen, "Health Reform and the Polls."

49 Greg Hitt and Janet Adamy, "Senate Passes Sweeping Health-Care Bill, 69–39 Vote is Landmark in Effort to Expand Insurance Coverage," Wall Street Journal, December 25, 2009.

50 David Espo and Erica Werner, "Democrats Plan to Fast-track Final Health Care Bill, Tactic Designed to Stymie GOP Opposition," Associated Press, January 5, 2010.

51 "C-SPAN Complains About Private Health Talks," Boston.com, January 5, 2010.

52 Penny Starr, "Joe Biden: 'We Have to Go Spend Money to Keep From Going Bankrupt,' " CNSNews.com, July 16, 2009.

53 "Naked Emperor News: 'Obama's Mother of All Political Lies and the Town Hall Mayhem it Caused," Breitbart.tv, August 10, 2009.

54 Sally Pipes, "The Truth Behind the Census Bureau's Insurance Figure," Washington Examiner, September 21, 2008.

55 Steven Ertelt, "Senate Passes Health Care Bill: Funds Abortions, Mandates Insurance Coverage," LifeNews.com, December 24, 2009.

56 "Exclusive: Coburn: Dem Health Plan Will Kill Americans," *Washington Times,* July 16, 2009.

57 Sally Pipes, *The Top Ten Myths of American Health Care* (San Francisco: Pacific Research Institute, 2008), p. 136.

58 Bob Hall, Book Review of Sally Pipes' "The Top Ten Myths of American Health Care," The Old Jarhead Blog, tartanmarine.blogspot.com, May 18, 2009.

59 Susan Easton, "Health Care Horror Stories Just in Time for Halloween," *Human Events,* October 19, 2009.

60 Michelle Malkin, "Cash for Cloture: Democare Bribe List, Pt. II," Michelle Malkin.com, December 21, 2009.

61 Betsy McCaughey, "10 Lumps of Coal in The Health Care Bill," Investors.com, December 23, 2009.

CHAPTER FOUR

1 "Obama: Iraq War 'Distracts' Military From Other Threats," FoxNews.com, July 15, 2008.

2 "Obama: U.S. Troops in Afghanistan Must Do More Than Kill Civilians," FoxNews.com, August 14, 2007.

3 Ibid.

4 Barack Obama, "Remarks of Senator Obama: The War We Need to Win," BarackObama.com, August 1, 2007.

5 "Obama Campaign Releases National TV Ad on New Leadership for a Changing World," BarackObama.com, July 16, 2008.

6 Jim Lobe, "U.S.: Diplomacy, Multilaterism Stressed by Obama Team," IPSNews .net, December 1, 2008.

7 Ian Jannetta, "Clinton Touts Foreign Policy Experience, Criticizes Obama During GW Speech," CBSNews.com, February 25, 2008.

8 Barack Obama, "Remarks of Senator Obama: The War We Need to Win," BarackObama.com, August, 1, 2007.

9 Ibid.

10 Ibid.

11 Claudia Rosett, "Obama the Appeaser?" Forbes.com, February 26, 2009.

12 Barack Obama, "Full Text of Obama's Berlin Speech," TPM Election Central, July 24, 2008.

13 Nile Gardiner, Ph.D., and Morgan Roach, "Barack Obama's Top 10 Apologies: How the President Has Humiliated a Superpower," Heritage.org, June 2, 2009.

14 Jeffrey Fleishmann, "Obama Launches Effort to 'Communicate' in Mideast," *Los Angeles Times,* January 28, 2009.

15 Mark Landler, "Clinton Says U.S. Feeds Mexico Drug Trade," *New York Times*, March 26, 2009.

16 Jonathan Weisman, Alistair McDonald, and Carrick Mollenkamp, "Obama Hits Resistance at G-20: In His First Turn on World Stage, President Faces Challenge From France, Germany," *Wall Street Journal,* April 2, 2009.

17 Transcript: Obama's G20 Press Conference, "The President Answered Questions From Reporters at the End of the G20 Summit in London," CBSNews.com, April 2, 2009.

18 Federal News Service, "Obama Holds Town Hall in Strasbourg, France," Washingtonpost.com, April 3, 2009.

19 Barack Obama, "Remarks By President Barack Obama," White House, April 5, 2009.

20 Barack Obama, "Remarks By President Obama to the Turkish Parliament," April 6, 2009.

21 Barack Obama, "Op-ed by President Barack Obama: 'Choosing a Better Future in the Americas,' " April 16, 2009, http://www.whitehouse.gov/the_press_office/Op -ed-by-President-Barack-Obama-Choosing-a-Better-Future-in-the-Americas/.

22 "On World Stage, Obama Uses Podium to Express Regret," FoxNews.com, May 12, 2009.

23 Major Garrett, "Obama Endures Ortega Diatribe," FoxNews.com, April 18, 2009.

24 L. Brent Bozell III, "Obama Welcomes America-Bashing," Creators Syndicate, April 21, 2009.

25 James Gordon Meek, "President Obama Tells CIA Not to Worry About Terror Memo Releases," New York *Daily News*, April 21, 2009.

26 Barack Obama, Speech at the National Archives, "Remarks by the President on National Security," May 21, 2009, http://www.whitehouse.gov/the_press _office/Remarks-by-the-President-On-National-Security-5-21-09/.

27 Ibid.

28 Karl Rove, "The President's Apology Tour," Opinion Journal, *Wall Street Journal,* April 23, 2009.

29 "BMD: What the Polish Papers Say," Leopolisblogspot.com, September 18, 2009.

30 Rove, "The President's Apology Tour."

31 Patrick Goodenough, "Muted Response from Obama Administration to Iran's Post-Election Ferment," CNSNews.com, June 15, 2009.

32 "Netanyahu Ready to Resume Mideast Peace Talks, Obama Tells Israeli Leader It's Time to Get Back to Negotiating Table," Associated Press, May 18, 2009.

33 "Ahmadinejad on Nuke Deadline: 'We Don't Care,' " FoxNews.com,, December 22, 2009.

34 Editorial, "Dead Deadline," Investors.com, January 6, 2010.

35 "Obama Extends Hand, But America's Critics Keep Fists Clenched," FoxNews .com, December 28, 2009.

36 Associated Press, "Text of Cheney's Speech on National Security," May 21, 2009.

37 Jonathan Dienst, "NYPD Commish: Nobody Asked Us About Hosting the 9/11 Trials," NBCNewYork.com, December 3, 2009.

38 Robert Spencer, "Al-Qaeda in the Arabian Peninsula Claims Responsibility for Flight 253 Attack," *Jihad Watch,* December 29, 2009.

39 Susan Jones, "Obama Describes Nigerian As 'Isolated Extremist,' Despite Ties to Yemen," CNSNews.com, December 29, 2009.

40 "U.S. Knew of Airline Terror Plot Before Christmas," FoxNews.com, December 30, 2009.

41 Jim Meyers, "Obama: U.S. Knew of Nigerian Terror Threat But Did Not Act," Newsmax.com, December 30, 2009.

42 Opinion, "Abdulmutallab in 50 Minutes," Opinionjournal.com, Wall Street Journal, January 26, 2010.

43 Victoria Toensing, "Trying Abdul Mutallab," The Corner, National Review Online, January 5, 2010.

44 Andy McCarthy, "Trying Abdul Mutallab," The Corner, National Review Online, January 5, 2010.

CHAPTER FIVE

1 Andrew Malcolm, "Barack Obama Wants to Be President of These 57 States," *Los Angeles Times,* May 9, 2008.

2 Editorial, "Bush's Evil Axis," Boston Globe, February 3, 2002.

3 "Former President Carter Speaks Out Against Bush's 'Axis of Evil,'" *Atlanta Journal Constitution,* February 21, 2002.

4 Arlene Getz with Catherine Ferguson, "Outside the U.S. Little Praise for Bush's State of the Union Speech," *Newsweek,* January 30, 2002.

5 "Bush Is Dogged by 'Axis of Evil' in Visit to Japan," *Los Angeles Times,* February 19, 2002.

6 David Talbot, "Axis of Stupidity," Salon.com, February 14, 2002.

7 Peter Goldman with Thomas M. DeFrank, Eleanor Clift and John J. Lindsay, James Doyle and John Walcott, "Not Very Happy Warriors," *National Affairs,* United States Edition, August 18, 1980.

8 Tom Wicker, "In the Nation; 2 Dangerous Doctrines," *New York Times,* March 15, 1983.

9 Walter Laqueur, "The Terrorism to Come," *Policy Review,* August and September 2004.

10 Amy Zalman, Ph.D., "Is Terrorism's Cause Poverty?" About.com.

11 Anthony Lewis, "Onward Christian Soldiers," *New York Times,* March 10, 1983.

12 Ronald Reagan, "A Time for Choosing," transcript at the website of the Miller Center for Public Affairs, University of Virginia, http://millercenter.org/scripps /archive/speeches/detail/3405.

13 Ed Rubenstein, "Introduction, the Real Reagan Record," *National Review,* August 31, 1992.

14 Alan Reynolds, "Upstarts and Downstarts, The Real Reagan Record," *National Review,* August 31, 1992.

15 U.S. Office of Management and Budget, *Budget of the United States Government, Fiscal Year 2001: Historical Tables,* February 2000, Table 1.3, p. 23; Peter B. Sperry, Ph.D., "The Real Reagan Economic Record: Responsible and Successful Fiscal Policy," Backgrounder #1414, Heritage Foundation, March 1, 2001.

16 William A. Niskanen and Stephen Moore, "Cato Policy Analysis No. 261, Supply-Side Tax Cuts and the Truth About the Reagan Economic Record," Cato Institute, October 22, 1996.

17 Paul Kengor, "Party of Life," National Review Online, April 22, 2004.

18 Ronald Reagan, "Remarks at the Annual Convention of the National Religious Broadcasters," January 30, 1984.

19 "Poll: Conservatives Most Dominant Political Group Among Americans," FoxNews.com, October 26, 2009.

20 "GOP Insiders Sour on Palin," Hotline On Call, *National Journal,* January 7, 2010.

21 Dick Armey, "End of the Revolution, Advice to Republicans: Don't Go Back and Check on a Dead Skunk," Opinion Journal, *Wall Street Journal,* November 9, 2006.

22 David Frum, *Comeback: Conservatism That Can Win Again* (New York: Doubleday, 2008), pp. 103-4.

23 Amanda B. Carpenter, "Obama More Pro-Choice Than NARAL," *Human Events,* December 26, 2006.

CHAPTER SIX

1 Dick Armey, "End of the Revolution, Advice to Republicans: Don't Go Back and Check on a Dead Skunk," Opinion Journal, *Wall Street Journal,* November 9, 2006.

2 Jeffrey B. Gayner, "The Contract with America: Implementing New Ideas in the U.S.," Heritage Lecture #549, Heritage Foundation, October 12, 1995.

3 Ibid.

4 Ibid.

5 Newt Gingrich, "Contract with America, 10 Year Anniversary, Celebrating a Decade of Republican Leadership in Congress," Newt.org, September 27, 2004.

6 Gayner, "The Contract with America."

7 Ibid.

8 R. W. Apple, Jr., ""The 104th Congress: The Overview; Republican Blitz Shakes Congress," *New York Times,* September 23, 1995.

9 Robert Reno, "Republicans Invent Warm, Fuzzy Names to Cover the Snarling Face of Their Ripper Legislation the GOP-Loves-You Laws," *San Jose Mercury News,* November 20, 1994.

10 Apple, "The 104th Congress."

11 Gayner, "The Contract with America."

12 Abraham McLaughlin, "GOP Set to Push Through Cut in Capital Gains Tax," *Christian Science Monitor,* December 19, 2004.

13 Michael Bauman, "The Dangerous Samaritans: How We Unintentionally Injure the Poor," *Imprimis,* Hillsdale College, 2008.

14 The Personal Responsibility and Work Opportunity Reconciliation Act and Associated Legislation, Summary of Welfare Reforms Made By Public Law 104–193, Committee on Ways and Means, U.S. House of Representatives, November 6, 1996.

15 Christine Kim and Robert Rector, "Welfare Reform Turns Ten: Evidence Shows Reduced Dependence, Poverty," WebMemo #1183, Heritage Foundation, August 1, 2006.

16 Ibid.

17 "Welfare Reform: Bringing Dignity to Millions (But Not to Bill Clinton)," United States Senate, Republican Policy Committee, August 5, 1999.

18 Robert Rector, "Bill Clinton Was Right," *Washington Post,* August 23, 2006.

19 "Under Fire, Democrat Retreats," *Washington Times,* September 11, 2006.

20 Governor Ronald Reagan, "The New Republican Party," Conservative Political Action Conference, Washington, DC, February 7, 1977.

CHAPTER SEVEN

1 Robert Rector and Katherine Bradley, "Stimulus Bill Abolishes Welfare Reform and Adds New Welfare Spending," WebMemo #2287, Heritage Foundation, February 11, 2009.

2 Paul M. Weyrich, "A 2006 Democratic Sweep and A Precursor to 2008?" Free Congress Commentary, August 1, 2006.

3 John Hinderaker, "Brand Damage," Powerlineblog.com, November 10, 2008.

4 John Fund, "Alaska's GOP Congressmen Are Bridge to Nowhere," *Wall Street Journal,* August 16, 2008.

5 Dick Armey, "End of the Revolution, Advice to Republicans: Don't Go Back and Check on a Dead Skunk," Opinion Journal, *Wall Street Journal,* November 9, 2006.

6 Peter Kirsanow, "New Black Panther Party Voter-Intimidation Case Dismissal, Part III," The Corner, National Review Online, August 11, 2009.

7 "Editorial: Letting Crooks and Illegals Vote," *Washington Times,* January 7, 2010.

CHAPTER EIGHT

1 Mark Tapscott, "New Media Leader Exposes Myth of Obama's 'Bottom-up' Internet-driven 2008 campaign," *Washington Examiner,* January 2, 2010.

2 "Tea Party Leader: 'We Are Turning Our Guns On' Moderate Republicans," Huffington Post, January 1, 2010.

3 Lydia Saad, "Conservatives Finish 2009 as No. 1 Ideological Group, Uptick Owing Largely to More Independents Calling Themselves Conservative," Gallup.com, January 7, 2010.

4 Associated Press, "Obama: 'Bitter' Comments Were Ill-Chosen," *USA Today,* April 13, 2008.

CHAPTER NINE

1 William Bradford, *Of Plymouth Plantation* (New York: Knopf, 1952), p. 121.

2 Milton Friedman, "Milton Friedman Takes Phil Donahue to School on Greed," The Patriot Room Blog, February 12, 2009.

3 Mark J. Perry, "Milton Friedman (Happy Birthday) Destroys Phil Donahue," Encyclopedia Britannica.com,, July 31, 2009.

4 "No More Screw-Ups," *Investor's Business Daily,* January 6, 2010.

5 Reagan, "The New Republican Party,"

6 Edwin Meese III, "The Meaning of the Constitution," Heritage Foundation, WebMemo #2616, September 16, 2009.

7 Alexander Hamilton, James Madison, John Jay, *The Federalist Papers* (New York, NY: Signet, 2003), p. 293.

8 Reagan, "The New Republican Party."

9 Ibid.

10 Ibid.

11 Ibid.

12 Ibid.

CHAPTER TEN

1 T.W. Farnham, "Social Security, Medicare Face Insolvency Sooner," *Wall Street Journal,* May 13, 2009.